DEMOCRACY IN
COSTA RICA

POLITICS IN LATIN AMERICA
A HOOVER INSTITUTION SERIES

General Editor, **Robert Wesson**

Copublished with Hoover Institution Press,
Stanford University, Stanford, California

DEMOCRACY IN COSTA RICA

Charles D. Ameringer

PRAEGER

PRAEGER SPECIAL STUDIES • PRAEGER SCIENTIFIC

Library of Congress Cataloging in Publication Data

Ameringer, Charles D., 1926–
    Democracy in Costa Rica.

    (Politics in Latin America)
    Bibliography: p.
    Includes index.
    1. Costa Rica—Politics and government—1948–
I. Title. II. Series.
F1548.A43   1982   306'.097286   82-9065
ISBN 0-03-062158-5   AACR2

*The Hoover Institution on War, Revolution and Peace,
founded at Stanford University in 1919 by the late President
Herbert Hoover is an interdisciplinary research center for
advanced study on domestic and international affairs in the
twentieth century. The views expressed in its publications
are entirely those of the authors and do not necessarily
reflect the views of the staff, officers, or Board of Overseers
of the Hoover Institution.*

Published in 1982 by Praeger Publishers
CBS Educational and Professional Publishing
a Division of CBS Inc.
521 Fifth Avenue, New York, New York 10175 U.S.A.

Printed in the United States of America

For my parents

EDITOR'S FOREWORD

Costa Rica is famed and important beyond its size and numbers (second smallest in Latin America) as a verdant oasis of democracy and political maturity in a desert of dictatorship and political violence. Except for a brief civil war in 1948,when the results of an election were called into question, Costa Rica has enjoyed since the 1890s almost perfect constitutional continuity rare in the Third World. Elections are fully free and fair, and since 1948 the opposition party has usually won. The *ticos*, as Costa Ricans call themselves, enjoy democratic procedures and take pride in their popular government. No other country of Latin America, perhaps none among the hundred-odd countries of the Third World, has so sound a democratic tradition.

Yet Costa Rica is not miraculously exempt from the problems of Central America. There are sharper class differences than usually admitted (although less than in other Latin American countries), and there may be a potential for violence beneath the relatively placid surface. The country has sunk into an economic morass from which it will be very difficult to lift itself for a long time, and which may call the admired political system into question. A disarmed and impoverished Costa Rica can no longer be confident of its tranquility and safety in its turbulent environment.

In this situation, it is fortunate that Professor Charles Ameringer has produced a thorough study of the Costa Rican way, bringing it forward to the election of Luis Alberto Monge, on whom the *ticos* have laid great hopes. If Costa Rican democracy should wither or be cast down, the outlook for democratic development in Latin America will be much darkened. On the other hand, Ameringer's study may reinforce our hope — which is the *ticos'* confidence — that their pleasant country can fulfill its promise.

Robert Wesson

PREFACE

This book is intended for all those who have ever wondered about the uniqueness of Costa Rica. This small Central American state has a reputation for peace and democracy that makes it a curiosity among the nations of Latin America. There is no simple explanation for why Costa Rica is different from its neighbors, and one feels pretentious in attempting to describe national character; but after more than 25 years of research, travel, and observation, I may be able to provide some insights. Where I have used the ideas and analyses of others, I have referred to them directly in the text, citing their works in full in the bibliography. I am indebted to friends in Costa Rica with whom I have discussed the Costa Rican idiosyncrasy at length — namely José Figueres, Benjamín Núñez, Rodrigo Carreras, Fernando Volio, Francisco Morales, and Samuel Stone. I am grateful to the Pennsylvania State University, particularly the Liberal Arts Research Office and the Institute for the Arts and Humanistic Studies, for enabling me to travel to Costa Rica over the years and to become familiar with its people.

CONTENTS

DEMOCRACY IN
COSTA RICA

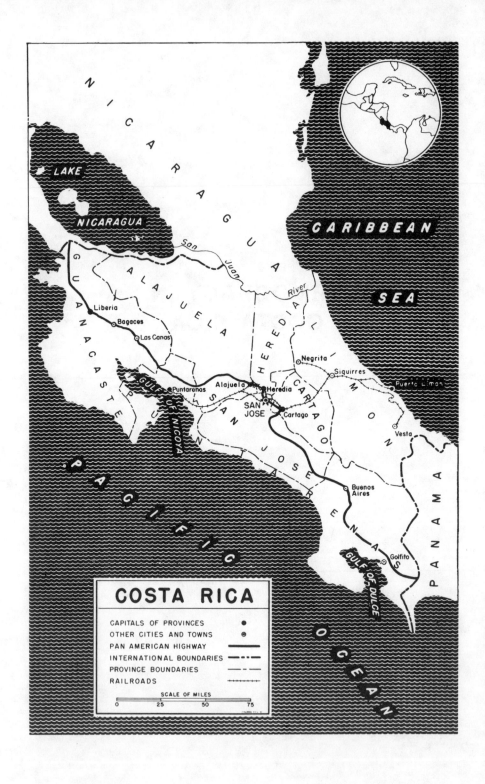

COSTA RICA

CAPITALS OF PROVINCES	●
OTHER CITIES AND TOWNS	⊚
PAN AMERICAN HIGHWAY	———
INTERNATIONAL BOUNDARIES	—·—·—
PROVINCE BOUNDARIES	—— —
RAILROADS	++++++

SCALE OF MILES

0   25   50   75

INTRODUCTION: A LA TICA

Costa Ricans, or *ticos*, as they call themselves, describe their country as one that produces good coffee and decent people. The description is appropriate. Costa Rica is a small country, smaller in total area than the state of West Virginia, and everyone is everyone else's cousin. They call themselves *ticos* because of their fondness for using the diminutive in speech, a practice designed to soften their expression and avoid giving offense. They do not like unpleasantness and shun extremes and fanaticism. Disputes are resolved *a la tica* — that is, the *tico* way: with civility and without rancor. It is their idiosyncrasy, their manner of being, and everything is adjusted to it. *Ticos* are essentially conservative, exhibiting a healthy skepticism and preferring, when confronted with change, to "think about it." They are indeed a decent people, and that may explain why their country is a democracy.

Ticos know that their democracy is not perfect, but they cherish their freedom; democracy is not merely a system of government, but a deep feeling. The system has worked long enough and well enough to have acquired legitimacy. *Ticos* enjoy free speech and a free press, and their electoral process is as unfettered and honest as any anywhere in the world. Every four years, they hold their *fiesta cívica*, (election) with noise and passion, but when the ballots, are cast and the votes counted, they accept the decision with grace and good humor. The transfer of power, even to the political opposition, which has been the case more often than not in the last 30 years, is carried out with dignity in civic ceremonies in the National Stadium. Critics of *tico* democracy describe these proceedings as mere trappings, complaining that there is a lack of meaningful participation in government among the popular classes and charging that the system inhibits change, rather than promoting it. It is true that in recent times, Costa Rica has experienced serious economic and social problems arising from the commerical cultivation of coffee and the rapid increase in population, which have placed severe strains upon the *tico* way; but it is also true that Costa Rica has achieved remarkable change, especially since the 1948 civil war, and has made steady progress toward economic and social justice. No one suggests that *tico* democracy is out of danger.

Essential to an understanding of *tico* democracy is the Costa Ricans' faith in education and distrust of militarism. It is a cliché that there are more schoolteachers than soldiers in Costa Rica, but it is one founded in reality. Patriotic holidays are observed with parades by schoolchildren, rather than by reviews of troops and military hardware. It is a standing joke that Costa Rica lacks sufficient firepower to give visiting heads of state a 21-gun salute. Almost one-third of the national budget is expended for primary and secondary education. Upon founding their nation, *ticos* determined that the people were sovereign and that the principal function of government was to educate the people to enable them to govern properly. With neither an external threat nor an indigenous population to subjugate, warfare and arms were not part of the colonial experience. Costa Rica achieved independence without bloodshed, so civilian authorities, not *caudillos* (military chieftains), formed the first government. The country's principal military hero is a peasant boy, Juan Santamaría, who sacrificed his life in the last century while defending Costa Rica against the adventurer William Walker. The national anthem extols Costa Rica's friendly soil and lovely flowers, with no reference to exploding shells or dying soldiers. The schoolteacher and civilian statesman represent Costa Rican democracy, but the picture is not complete without the yeoman farmer.

Alberto Cañas (1978) describes the small proprietor as the backbone of Costa Rican democracy. Although current statistics indicate that the yeoman farmer is fast disappearing, and Cañas fears that Costa Rican democracy may be losing its economic base, some observers, such as James Busey (1962), maintain that land ownership is still widespread in Costa Rica. But even granting that land distribution is a serious problem in contemporary Costa Rica, it is a fact that the expansion of the coffee *fincas* (estates) began only a decade or so before the mid-nineteenth century, whereas the system of small, family farms had by then existed for three centuries. The experience of the rural *tico* had been one of individualism and egalitarianism, which could not be erased easily from the culture, even with significant economic change. Moreover, when the process of land engrossment began, the population of Costa Rica was small — it was only 65,000 in 1821 and it was barely twice that number 50 years later — so that labor was scarce. Even dispossessed, the rural population was free to move, which led the owners of *fincas* to compete for workers and to treat them well. The new coffee *finca* arose under circumstances quite different from those of the Hispanic *latifundia* (large landed estate). Its work force was not made up of a conquered race or of imported slaves held in inferior status by the institutionalized tyrany of a ruling class, but consisted of persons accustomed to being free and who had the same cultural heritage as the emerging coffee baron. Clearly, the position of the former small proprietor deteriorated, particularly as insecurity accompanied the loss of land; but the relationship between peasant and *patrón* was close — so much so that, as Samuel Stone (1975) observes, they frequently mixed socially. The *patrón* was not an absentee landlord. He attended the peasants' *fiestas*, and they his, and the peasants danced with the wife of the *patrón*. It would be erroneous to say that Costa Rica is a classless society, but the factor of cultural homogeneity served to make less likely the use of repression, even as the gap between rich and poor widened.

Cultural homogeneity provides another element, and a pervasive one, in the framework of *tico* democracy. The majority of Costa Ricans are described as white. One encounters the interpretation that this whiteness accounts for Costa Rican democracy, which is as false as it is racist. It is more reasonable to affirm that where you do not have a system based upon the domination of one race or culture by another, you are more likely to evolve a freer society and a more stable order, particularly if there is also a lack of wealth, as was the case in Costa Rica before the coffee era. On the other hand, *ticos* have exhibited racial prejudice. They are proud of their whiteness and they tend to look down upon the Indian and *mestizo* populations of their Central American neighbors. Within Costa Rica, the Indian population is regarded as too small to worry about, and the black population is concentrated in Limón province on the Caribbean coast. The blacks of Limón do not share the opinion that Costa Rica is a just society. At one time, they were not free to migrate to the Meseta Central (Central Plateau) in search of work. Even today, they remain physically isolated, and Limón is one of the most depressed regions of Costa Rica. Limón's black population of approximately 33,000 constitutes a challenge, but not a threat, to the majority on the Meseta.

Political power has always resided on the Meseta Central and it was exercised for a long time by the descendants of the *conquista-dores.* Stone (1975) reports that 33 presidents of the republic (out of a total of 45) were descended from just three *conquistador* families; he believes that "*sangre*" (blood) is the principal cohesive factor in Costa Rican society. During the colonial period and for the first century of the republic, members of this class governed and enjoyed social status, but, until the coffee era, they were not affluent. By the time coffee made some of the class wealthy, their own spirit of service, as well as the essential egalitarianism of the *tico* population, had been formed. Stone perceives a "delicate balance" between elitism and egalitarianism in Costa Rican society. Moreover, not all descendants of the *conquistadores* were governors — some were smugglers and outcasts — and not all became coffee barons, particularly second and third sons who had to find another livelihood. The scarcity of labor promoted class interdependence, which was reinforced by the fact that the *beneficios* (coffee-processing plants), even if connected with the large producers, also relied upon the crop of small cultivators, in order to operate at full capacity. Today, with the members of the *conquistador* class dispersed along the political, social, and economic spectrums, political rivals are frequently blood relatives. One is not surprised by the high quality, if conservative nature, of the Costa Rican leadership historically, nor by the disposition of *ticos* to resolve affairs *a la tica.* The existence of a "*leyenda blanca*" ("white legend") about Costa Rica is easy to understand, but legends may be misleading and have a very slight relationship with reality.

Although *ticos* are proud of their democracy, they resent hearing, especially from North Americans, that they are peaceful and stable and "just like us." *Ticos* are aware that they have immense economic and social problems and they are concerned about the ability of their democratic institutions to deal with them effectively. A cartoon by Hugo Díaz (1978) sums up this sentiment well: Two affluent gentlemen walking along the street pass a poor man in rags who is rummaging through a garbage can; the man shouts, "I am hungry," and the gentlemen observe, "One good thing about this country is its unrestricted freedom of expression." The National Planning Office (OFIPLAN),* in its 1980 study, lamented that, despite Costa Rica's democratic system, broad sectors of the population were on the periphery of the decision-making process. It reported that 15.8 percent of the work force was unemployed and that income distribution was unequal: In 1974, 10 percent of the richest families absorbed 36 percent of the total income, whereas the poorest 50 percent accounted for only 21.3 percent. Other studies conclude that one-quarter of the population lives in poverty (see Table 1).

The most serious economic and social problems have arisen in relatively recent times. *Tico* democracy was formed at a time when, indeed, everyone knew everyone else. As late as 1948, there were only 800,000 persons in Costa Rica, but with the population doubling every 20 years, it stands at over 2 million today (see Table 2). Although population growth slowed a bit in the sixties and early seventies, it is estimated that there will be 3.5 million persons in Costa Rica by the year 2000. Moreover, today, 61 percent of the population is concentrated on the Meseta Central — an area of approximately 770 square miles, out of a national total of 19,600 — and OFIPLAN affirms that at the present rate, 81 percent of the population will reside there in 2000. Already, San José, the principal city, is beset with urban sprawl and blight, and the deterioration of the quality of life, including air, water, and noise pollution, alcoholism, drug abuse, and a rising crime rate. In the countryside, deforestation and other wasteful practices have done immeasurable ecological damage.

---

*For a full list of government ministries and agencies, in English and in Spanish, see pp. 42-44.

TABLE 1
Percentage of Poor Families in Costa Rica, Urban and Rural, 1973

	Methodologies*				
	I	II	IIIc	IIIm	IIIl
Total Country	24.5	23.0	35.6	44.1	51.4
Urban	13.8	13.3	22.1	28.5	35.0
Rural	31.9	29.2	44.9	54.8	62.8

*Definition of poor families.

I: Families with an annual per capita income less than ₡1,100 ($165.42), plus those that simultaneously represent a large number of members, low levels of education, and poor condition of dwelling (1973: ₡6.64=$1.00).

II: Idem I, excluding farm families that have ten hectares of land or five hectares of arable land.

IIIc: Families with an annual per capita income less than ₡1,100, excluding farm families with 20 or more hectares of land.

IIIm: Families with an annual per capita income less than ₡1,400 ($210.53), excluding farm families with 20 hectares of land.

IIIl: Families with an annual per capita income less than ₡1,700 ($255.64), excluding farm families with 20 or more hectares of land.

Source: OFIPLAN, *Plan Nacional de Desarrollo, 1979 – 1982,* (San José, 1980).

Some critics are quick to blame foreign influences and consumerism for the ills plaguing Costa Rica today, and they call for the restoration of the "old values." Samuel Rovinski (1977) deplores the baneful influence of television, with its imported U.S. programs and emphasis upon violence and melodrama, plus its control by those selling chewing gum, deodorants, alcohol, and tobacco. Alberto Cañas (1978) is also worried about the effects of pop culture upon Costa Rican youth, noting that university students wear T-shirts "made in U.S.A.," with, ironically, Che Guevara's face imprinted upon them. Young *ticos* prefer rock music, to the extent, write Mavis, Richard, and Karen Biesanz (1979), that in 1975 Costa Rica passed a law requiring 25 percent of the music in juke boxes to be "national compositions performed by *ticos.*"

Costa Rica is clearly a society in transition. Modernization, urbanization, and population growth are placing strains upon *tico*

TABLE 2
Population Growth, 1925-80

Year	Population (in thousands)	Average Annual Percentage Growth Rate
1925	458.5	
		2.0
1930	506.2	
		2.4
1935	569.9	
		2.5
1940	644.8	
		2.7
1945	736.7	
		3.1
1950	858.2	
		3.5
1955	1,023.9	
		3.8
1960	1,236.1	
		3.6
1965	1,482.4	
		3.1
1970	1,732.1	
		2.5
1975	1,964.9	
		3.2
1980	2,286.0	

Source: Universidad Nacional, Sexto Seminario Nacional de Demografia, *Informe* (Heredia, Costa Rica, 1976, updated).

democracy. Costa Rica's reputation as the "Switzerland of the Americas" is being tested. Its political process remains free, and its people enjoy the most complete freedoms found anywhere, but more is expected. The system is being called upon increasingly to resolve the issues of social justice and economic opportunity, and critics say it cannot respond. The complaint is widespread that the huge state bureaucracy constitutes a powerful interest group, which siphons off too many resources and leaves too little for attending to the needs of society, for which it was created in the first place. The welfare state, in place since the early 1950s, created a middle class of bureaucrats who allegedly are insensitive to the misery of the poor. A related complaint says that Costa Rica actually has too much democracy: that the system of checks and balances has weakened the presidency; and that the further decentralization of power within the executive branch itself has, as Charles Denton (1971) writes, immobilized the state and is frustrating its ability to promote change. If too much of a good thing is thwarting reform and if the beneficiaries of the system are too few, then *tico* democracy is in trouble. The system broke down in 1948, and another crisis may be shaping up. It serves no purpose to be alarmist, but it does not help to accept unflinchingly the myth of Costa Rican democracy. In studying Costa Rica, one ought to follow the example of the *ticos* themselves — the *tico* way — by being skeptical and staying cool.

2

THE NATURE AND DEVELOPMENT
OF TICO DEMOCRACY

Scholars generally agree that the foundations of Costa Rica's democracy may be discovered in the colonial experience. Unlike many of the New World colonies of Spain, Costa Rica lacked the resources to support aristocratic-autocratic institutions. Its name was the expression of wishful thinking, not reality. Costa Rica lacked sufficient mineral wealth to attract the gold seekers, and its indigenous population was too small to permit the establishment of large landed estates. The settlers who came had to work the land by themselves, limiting the size of holdings to what they and their families could manage. Even the founder of the colony, Juan Vásquez de Coronado, worked his own plot, in order not to perish. Moreover, Costa Rica was isolated from the centers of Spanish bureaucratic control. It was separated from Guatemala, the seat of the captaincy general, by great distance and tortuous terrain. Poverty, cultural homogeneity, and isolation were indeed the principal characteristics of the colonial experience.

Given these circumstances, Costa Rica evolved a society quite distinct from that of other Spanish colonies in America. Although local crown officials exercised authority, the colony provided little opportunity for the rise of a leisure class, and the governors were no better off than the governed. Even the church was poor, and the colonists rarely attended mass, because they lacked proper clothing and were ashamed to be seen in public. The colonists, out of necessity, preferred to live on separate farms, and only when they were compelled to do so, at the insistence of the clergy, did they build on town lots. Cartago, the colonial capital, was a politico-religious center, lacking any significant economic base. The second town, Heredia, had similar origins, being established to promote a second congregation. Money was so scarce that what little trade existed was conducted by barter, although cacao beans were sometimes used as a medium of exchange. With work needed to survive, the stereotype of the Spaniard refusing to work with his hands did not fit in with Costa Rican society.ᴸA simplicity of life style, a fierce individualism, and an egalitarian spirit became the hallmarks of *tico* existence. These traits were reinforced by the factor of cultural homogeneity, which is a better term than "racial purity," because, early on, given the fact that male immigrants outnumbered women, there was a degree of miscegenation. Nonetheless, there was no large subjugated population, and the colonists were too poor to import slaves, which meant that a military caste did not arise. It would be false to affirm that class distinctions did not exist, particularly on the political and social levels, but it is not contradictory to conclude that a rural democracy was evolving in the Costa Rican colony. Its basis was the presence of the small proprietor, who was proudly self-reliant and too poor and little inclined to support any significant governmental apparatus.

Although the colony was isolated, it was compact. The Central Plateau, or Central Valley, is surrounded by mountain ranges. On the valley floor, averaging 3,000 feet above sea level, the colonists' farms were scattered about, but the area itself is a well-defined geographical unit, with good soil, a pleasant climate, and adequate rainfall. Beyond the mountains, to the north, east, and south, the rainfall is heavy, the jungles are dense, and the land is poorly drained, especially along the Caribbean coast. The climate is drier in the northwest, in Guanacaste province, toward the Nicaraguan border. Because of the sparsity and poverty of the population, there was little outmigration. The colony could not support a frontier, the absence of which explained further the lack of a military element. The colony was not only isolated from the rest of Central America, but was isolated within Costa Rica itself. The *ticos* were on their own, making out as well as they could.

In view of the fact that the Costa Rican colony offered only isolation and hardship, why did a number of spanish *hidalgos* (noblemen) go there, particularly without an official position? Samuel Stone (1975) speculates that many of them may have been Sephardic Jews; although they had been converted to Catholicism by the fifteenth century and had achieved the status of *hidalgo*, many Sephardic Jews fled Spain in the fifteenth and sixteenth centuries, in the face of a new wave of anti-Semitism and the revival of the Inquisition. If this were the case, and Stone suspects that it is so, it might explain the particular nature of the Spanish *hidalgos* in Costa Rica. It might explain why they welcomed isolation; why they were closely knit (as a group that had faced, and might again face, persecution); why, though they were Catholics, they were unusually tolerant; and even why they were industrious, not afraid of hard work, and willing to get their hands dirty. This class, as Stone calls it, provided leadership and governance, but lacked an economic underpinning to distinguish it from the rest of the colonists.

During the colonial period, the members of the *conquistador* class underwent the first in a series of divisions, somewhat like an amoeba that reproduces itself though a process of cell division. According to Stone, some of the dons resented the narrow economic policies of the Spanish crown, as enforced by Guatemala, and engaged in illicit trade. These contrabandists were, in effect, rebels and formed the basis for liberal thought in the colony. Even though they possessed the *sangre*, they were classified as "undesirables" by the peninsular authorities in Cartago and, in 1755, were banished and forced to relocate about 20 miles to the west, on the other side of the Ochomogo Height, in the present location of the city of San José. Rodolfo Cerdas (1975) notes that Cartago and Heredia remained centers of conservative thought and bureaucratic control, with a closed or domestic economy, whereas San José and its satellite, Alajuela, became agrocommercial centers, engaged in smuggling, (particularly tobacco), and exhibited an open, adventurous spirit. At the time of independence, there were really two Costa Ricas: the closed, self-sufficient, conservative society of Cartago and Heredia, with its closer ties to Spanish institutions, including the church; and the open, liberal society of San José and Alajuela, with its firmer commercial base and emerging middle class.

Independence came to Costa Rica virtually by default. The *ticos* had almost no part in the separation of the captaincy general of Guatemala from Spain, nor in the subsequent separation of it from Mexico and the formation of the United Provinces of Central America. All these actions were performed without bloodshed, which explains still further the lack of military experience in Costa Rica. Of the 28 signatories of the Act of Independence, Stone (1975) relates, 23 were closely related by blood. Distinct from the other states of Central America, where conservatives and liberals were separatists and unionists, respectively, the *tico* liberals promoted Costa Rica's secession from the Central American federation. According to Stone, the exiles and smugglers of San José "engendered the majority of the liberal thinkers of the first years of the Republic." Braulio Carrillo was foremost among these.

Carrillo had been the governor of the province in 1835 and, after Costa Rica's secession from the federation, remained as first president of the new republic until 1842. Even though the class was split, the so-called dynasty of the *conquistadores* continued to dominate the affairs of the republic, providing the overwhelming majority of presidents and deputies (congressmen) until well into the middle of the twentieth century, according to Stone (1975). Carrillo, however, fortified the ascendancy of the liberal branch by moving the capital of Costa Rica to San José, favoring its open, middle-class outlook as opposed to the traditional, colonial orientation of Cartago. He, in effect, also recognized that San José had become the economic center. Carrillo placed heavy emphasis upon education, believing that there could be no republic without the education of the people, and his liberal leanings affected even the social sphere. He prohibited mills from grinding cane from seven in the evening until five in the morning, because of the higher incidence of accidents in the evening and nighttime hours. Cerdas (1975) praises Carrillo as the "creator of Costa Rican nationality" and for "establishing the basis of Costa Rican liberal democracy."

Throughout the colonial period, because of its poverty, Costa Rica made little advancement in cultural matters, particularly in literature. Under the guidance of Carrillo and other precursors, the daily press helped overcome this deficiency in part by providing a means for the expression and dissemination of ideas. Costa Rica acquired its first printing press in 1830, and newspapers became the principal vehicle for political, educational, and cultural development. Because of the prevailing political freedom, the press enjoyed freedom of expression; and freedom of the press became another element of *tico* democracy — an important consideration, given the economic changes that occurred.

Economic change accompanied the birth of the republic. During the colonial period, the *conquistador* class had searched in vain for a means to enrich itself. After 1830, the activities of a German immigrant, Jorge Stiepel, led Carrillo to believe that coffee production might provide the answer. He took measures to encourage its cultivation, including making the planting of coffee trees a condition for the acquisition of land, which set an early precedent for the role of the Costa Rican state as an economic promoter. At first, because of the lack of an outlet on the Caribbean, the trade with other states was modest, being limited principally to Chile, but beginning in 1843, the situation changed. In that year, an English sea captain, William Le Lacheur, in command of the *Monarch*, arrived at the port of Puntarenas from Seattle, with a load of pelts. He was looking for ballast for his return voyage to Liverpool and arranged to take on approximately 500,000 pounds of coffee, promising to pay upon his return. He kept his word; the Liverpool connection had been made, and a new era had begun. The so-called coffee miracle transformed Costa Rica from the poorest colony in Central America to its richest and most progressive state (see Table 3).

The successful coffee planters enlarged their holdings. Land values on the Meseta soared, inducing many small proprietors to sell out. Others abandoned their farms, attracted by the relatively high wages of the coffee *fincas*. Still others lost their land, unable to compete in the new environment of commerical agriculture. In an economy just emerging from barter, credit facilities were lacking, and farmers mortgaged their land with the *beneficios*, which provided few safeguards against foreclosure. Coffee took over the economy, and the *ticos*, with their eyes wide open, went down the road to monoculture, with its cruel surprise lying in wait. Farmers, even those who did not want to, had no choice but to produce the "*grano*

TABLE 3
Various Social and Economic Indicators Comparing Costa Rica with its Central American Neighbors

	Population, 1980 (in thousands)	Area (square miles)	Percent of National Budget Spent on Education, 1977	Literacy, 1975 (percent)	Death Rate among Children of 1-4 Years of Age, 1970 (per thousand inhabitants)	Life Expectancy at Birth, 1975-80	Inhabitants per Doctor, 1968-71
Costa Rica	2,286	19,695	32.7	89	4.0	69.7	1,804
El Salvador	4,813	8,260	22.8	59	14.5	62.2	5,101
Guatemala	7,100	42,042	16.0	48	30.0	57.8	4,498
Honduras	3,595	43,277	19.1	45*	20.0	53.1	4,085
Nicaragua	2,733	57,000	13.0	52	18.4	52.9	2,014

	Percent of Population with Electric Lighting, 1973	Percent of Population with Drinking Water, 1975		Telephones, 1976		Length of Roads, 1975 (in kilometers)	
		Urban	Rural	in thousands	per hundred inhabitants	Total	Paved
Costa Rica	66.4	100	56	127	6.2	24,724	1,939
El Salvador	34.0	89	28	60	1.4	10,975	1,408
Guatemala	22.1	85	14	53†	1.0†	13,625	2,638
Honduras	17.0	100	10	20	.7	6,595	1,327
Nicaragua	45.0	100	14	55	2.5	17,526	1,597

*In 1961.
†In 1973.

Source: Adapted from James W. Wilkie (ed.). Statistical Abstract of Latin America, vol. 20 (Los Angeles: UCLA Latin American Center Publications, 1980).

de oro" (the golden bean). A heartless cycle took charge. Coffee raised the costs of farming, and only coffee could produce the revenue to meet the increased costs. As Mitchell Seligson (1980) notes, coffee proved to be "the aristocracy's salvation and the peasantry's ruination." By 1883, landless laborers constituted 71 percent of the rural population. But in a time of boom and expansion, this statistic did not necessarily mean misery.

Moreover, the dramatic change in the nature of Costa Rica's economy, from the colony to the republic, was not accompanied by the loss of political freedom. The individualistic, egalitarian nature of Costa Rican society had already been fixed, and even the new coffee barons exhibited the liberal disposition of the Costa Rican people. They sprang from the group that had attacked the conservativism and traditionalism of Cartago. Those who occupied the presidency were among the foremost liberal thinkers of the day. José María Castro Madriz, member of the class, coffee planter, and twice president, affirmed that the "greatest evil was ignorance" (Barahona, 1971) and that without education, there could be no progress. He advocated public education, freedom of the press, and religious freedom. Liberalism in Costa Rica, as in much of Latin America at that time, meant, above all else, anticlericalism. The coffee planters of San José opened the University of Santo Tomás at midcentury and dedicated it to rationalism and positivism, rejecting the scholasticism of the church fathers and Catholic philosophers, to which the older universities of León (Nicaragua) and San Carlos (Guatemala) still clung. Bruno Carranza, provisional president in 1870, added (Barahona, 1971) that all freedoms were important and had to be enjoyed together – specifically, religious freedom, political freedom, and economic freedom.

The *tico* leaders equated economic freedom with economic liberalism. In the absence of the feudalistic-style societies existing in other parts of Latin America, they encountered less resistance in the promotion of capitalism. José María Montealegre, president in 1859, coffee baron, and bluest of the blue bloods, had resided in England for 12 years, where he acquired a strong admiration for English capitalism. He looked upon liberal capitalism as the most effective means for achieving economic progress, which he regarded as essential for overcoming poverty and backwardness. Consistent with this belief, Montealegre promoted education, in order to prepare the people for commerce and eventual industrial development. He stressed, specifically, scientific and professional education. But this injection of the ideas of laissez-faire capitalism into Costa Rican society had its dark side as well. The coffee barons increasingly used their political supremacy to promote their own economic well-being. For the first time, political power was being used to promote narrow interests. With rich rewards at stake, the coffee barons fought among themselves, doing violence to the peaceful political process, with the rivalry between the Montealegre and Mora families becoming particularly fierce. This resort to force led to Costa Rica's first dictatorship.

Colonel Tomás Guardia, serving first as an agent of the rival coffee barons, seized power for himself in 1870 and dominated political affairs until his death 12 years later. Suffering a political eclipse, the coffee planters came to appreciate *tico* democracy, particularly civilian rule, during the time they lost it. Guardia displayed a degree of the positivist philosophy then in vogue in Latin America, although Luis Barahona (1971) suggests that Costa Ricans lacked the maturity to understand positivism and that, for them, it amounted to little more than "a pure admiration of the sciences." Nonetheless, Guardia promoted the familiar order and material progress as solutions to society's ills and undertook the construction of a railroad from the Meseta to the Caribbean.

This project, designed to facilitate the marketing of coffee in Europe, had an unforeseen result. Minor C. Keith, a young, enterprising North American, who eventually acquired the contract to carry out Guardia's dream, used the railroad to create his own fortune, but in bananas, not coffee. While the railroad was being constructed from Limón to the Meseta, Keith began transporting bananas, in order to provide revenue and prevent bankruptcy. First, he purchased available stems; then he acquired lands to produce his own crop. He found it difficult to lure labor from the Meseta, owing to the relatively high wages there and the unhealthful conditions of the Caribbean lowland, so he imported Jamaican blacks to help build the railroad and work on his plantations. Within 20 years, he had amassed a fortune, having helped to found the United Fruit Company and acquired a sobriquet, "the uncrowned king of Central America." Bananas provided Costa Rica with a totally different kind of economic enterprise. Whereas coffee was an integral part of the national economy, being a thoroughly *tico* product in its cultivation, processing, financing, and marketing, banana production was a foreign enterprise, being linked more to the U.S. fruit centers in Boston and New Orleans than to San José. It was an enclave economy, quite separate from the rest of the nation, with an alien work force (English-speaking, Protestant blacks) and with little economic impact on the Meseta. For a long time, bananas were not in the mainstream of *tico* society, nor did the politicians on the Meseta concern themselves much with the conditions of the black laborers on the plantations of "*la frutera*" (the fruit company: United Fruit). As long as the enterprises of Keith and his successors provided some revenue to Costa Rica through taxes, they were not bothered a great deal.

In the meantime, on the Meseta, following their first, serious experience with a dictatorship, the coffee elites demonstrated greater self-restraint with respect to the exercise of political power. Moreover, having lost their dominant position, even temporarily, they found it difficult to restore conditions to their former state. The further differentiation of the *conquistador* class itself compounded the situation. As the coffee economy expanded, greater division of labor took place, and Costa Rican society became more complex and pluralistic. The coffee planters, for the purpose of maintaining their lands intact and for the greater efficiency of larger holdings, followed the practice of bequeathing the land to the eldest son only. He was expected to take care of his sisters and younger brothers, but he alone was the master of the estate. What happened, in practice, was that the less-favored sons left the *finca* to pursue careers elsewhere, mainly in the liberal professions and in managerial and commercial activities connected with the coffee economy. Constituting an emerging middle class, they entered politics as a means of promoting their interests, hoping to strengthen electoral democracy, in order to compete more effectively with their older brothers, on the one hand, and prevent another Guardia-style regime, on the other.

This new element was fiercely democratic, but not at all antagonistic to the laissez-faire economic order. It concentrated its efforts upon strengthening *tico* democracy, which, during the administration of Próspero Fernández (1882-85), took the form of educational reform and a reinvigorated anticlericalism. Expressing the view that there must be absolute freedom of thought and that the aim of education is truth, Fernández and his minister of education, Mauro Fernández, advocated full separation of church and state and enacted the most sweeping reforms in Costa Rican history up to that time. The Liberal Laws of 1884 established free, compulsory secular education and, in other measures, expelled the Jesuit order, limited religious processions, permitted work on holy days, declared marriage a civil contract, permitted divorce, and secularized cemeteries. These reforms further diminished the influence of the Catholic church in Costa Rican affairs, even though it had never been powerful in a political sense and it remained the dominant religion. The liberal reformers also closed the University of Santo Tomás in 1888, on the grounds that it was elitist and had fallen under Jesuit control. The university remained closed until 1940, forcing Costa Ricans to go abroad to study. Only the law school continued to function, resulting in, as the Biesanzes (1979) note, "a nation of lawyers."

The activities and aggressiveness of the reformers resulted in 1889 in the first truly contested presidential election in Costa Rica. Rival candidates for the presidency made popular appeals for votes and engaged in an election that was neither rigged nor decided beforehand. The liberals were hampered by the fact that the suffrage was limited by property and literacy qualifications and that presidents were elected indirectly, but this election marked the beginning of greater popular participation in politics. The candidates even represented two distinct parties, the Liberal Progressive and the Democratic Constitutional, although until that time and for 50 years afterward, political parties were usually little more than labels and electoral vehicles for a particular personality. Costa Rican politics were highly personalistic, reflecting the individualistic character of *ticos*. As the victorious candidate, José Joaquín Rodríguez, remarked, "In Costa Rica, there is not, nor has there ever been, what in politics is called an organized party." (Rodríguez Vega, 1971) Nonetheless, out of this election arose an organization that, although short-lived, had the characteristics of a political party in that it was not based on personality alone. Ironically, it sprang from the Catholic church's reaction against the anticlerical laws of 1884, and not from the liberals themselves, who comprised the so-called generation of 1888.

The Catholic Union Party functioned during the 1890s and represented the antiliberal Catholic viewpoint. Barahona (1971) points out that Costa Rica lacked a serious center of religious study and thought and that, as a result, except for "a few priests," doctrinaire Catholicism never existed in Costa Rica. Even more noteworthy, he remarks, was the "intellectual poverty"of Catholics in those times, with reference to political and social affairs. Among the exceptions was Bishop Bernardo Augusto Thiel, a German schooled in France and Germany, who led the opposition to the Liberal Laws of 1884 and wrote that "lay education violates the principle of freedom of conscience" (Barahona, 1971). However, Bishop Thiel focused his attacks more upon social injustices arising from the laissez-faire economy than upon the political reforms of the liberals. In a pastoral letter of 1893, he called upon the state to fix a "just salary" for workers and artisans and criticized the huge fortunes of the coffee elites (Barahona, 1971). Thus, whereas the liberals attacked the church as reactionary and took measures to strip it of its privileges and influence, the position of the church leaders was actually more progressive in the economic and social spheres. Although this initiative had little success at the time, it was a harbinger of the role the Catholic church would play in the future. For the time being, the leadership of the nation belonged to the generation of 1888.

The generation of 1888 dominated Costa Rican political affairs for almost 50 years, represented especially by the so-called Olympians, Cleto González Víquez and Ricardo Jiménez Oreamuno, who occupied the presidency for 20 of the 30 years between 1906 and 1936. Don Cleto served two terms: in 1906-10 and 1928-32; and Don Ricardo held the office three times: in 1910-14, 1924-28, and 1932-36. These leaders were classic representatives of nineteenth-century liberalism, standing for universal suffrage, freedom of expression, and absolute separation of church and state. They were honest and capable administrators, running a modest state apparatus in the belief that government should defend individual liberty and not interfere with it. Their commitment to free enterprise won the support of the coffee barons, while the popular classes venerated them as new patriarchs, who possessed the civic virtues of honor and integrity, which *ticos* traditionally valued more than programs. They were highly personalistic leaders, preferring the building of schools and bridges to parties and institutions, but the peace and tranquillity they gave Costa Rica had an old smell to it and led ultimately to stagnation. In time, their failure to deal with economic and social ills caught up with them, although they, themselves, contributed to the eventual clamor for change.

Don Ricardo, in particular, believed in public education, and courted popular support for his leadership. When he ran for president for the first time in 1910, he made a special appeal to the rural sectors. After his election, Jiménez gave more power to the municipalities — expecially in the selection of deputies for the national Congress — which undermined the political monopoly theretofore exercised by Cartago and San José. Stone (1975) points out that this did not necessarily mean more popular government, but that it did result in further differentiation of the ruling class, because the so-called *gamonal* — well-to-do peasants making up a rural elite — obtained a share of national political power. By 1920, he notes, new surnames appeared on the roster of the national Congress. During his first presidency, Don Ricardo also enacted the reform establishing the direct election of the president. Although Jiménez valued democracy as a process for changing the governors, he believed in the function of the civilizing state as a means of changing the governed. His campaign against illiteracy had the effect of extending the suffrage, because, whereas 90 percent of the population had been illiterate during the nineteenth century, this figure had been reduced to 50 percent by 1928, making more persons eligible to vote. In that same year, as a result of Don Ricardo's efforts, Costa Ricans exercised the privilege of the secret ballot for the first time, further reducing the control by the elites. Therefore, the liberal patriarchs oversaw a process of democratization, which, along with other changes in society, proved their undoing.

The election of 1914, which had been scheduled as the first direct election of the president, ironically resulted in the choice of a minority president and compromise candidate. When none of three candidates for president obtained a majority of the votes cast, the election had to be decided by the Congress, which chose Alfredo González Flores, a dark horse, who had not been on the original ballot. Personalities played a dominant role in this election, but, when Máximo Fernández, the candidate with the most votes, could not carry the day, he managed to install González Flores, one of his leaders from Heredia. Although González Flores represented the liberal politics of the times, he proved more sensitive to economic and social issues. The population of Costa Rica was increasing rapidly — it had tripled since 1865, reaching approximately 360,000 by 1914 — and the nation was beginning to feel the effects of monoculture, with declining coffee prices and increasing dependence upon imported foodstuffs. In fact, coffee prices fell 50 percent between 1894 and 1901, making it necessary to grow more to earn less, and further reducing the acreage in food crops. González Flores wanted to institute an income tax, in order to require the rich to provide more for the poor, but the coffee oligarchy balked. He also had the misfortune to have to deal with the economic dislocations caused by World War I.

When European markets for coffee were cut off, Costa Rica sought to increase exports to the United States. The *ticos* had some success in this endeavor, marking the beginning of closer economic ties with the United States, but the decline in imports, caused by the worldwide lack of manufactured goods in wartime, resulted in monetary inflation and a decrease in government revenue from customs. Moreover, because of the uncertain economic conditions and the weakness of the *colón* (₡) in international money markets, the coffee barons tended to leave large portions of their earnings in dollars in U.S. banks. González Flores attempted to curb this capital flight through exchange regulations and to increase government revenue by raising taxes on coffee exports. He also undertook to provide credits to small farmers and to cut government costs by reducing the salaries of public employees, including schoolteachers. Not in a strong position from the start, he lost whatever political base he had when Don Cleto, Don Ricardo, and Máximo Fernández attacked him and his policies, leaving the coffee barons free to plot his ouster. Later generations praised González Flores as a statesman and precursor of economic and social change, but in his time, his popularity hit bottom and he had few defenders. Using the pretext that he intended to seek reelection and, thus, violate the sacred principle that no president should succeed himself, the minister of defense, Colonel Federico Tinoco, and his brother, Joaquín, staged a coup in January 1917, removing González Flores from office and establishing Costa Rica's second military dictatorship.

The Tinoco dictatorship constituted a serious threat to Costa Rican democracy, but it proved to be an aberration, and, in addition, the *ticos* received relief from the outside. The Tinoco brothers set up a tyrannical regime, subjecting *ticos* to arbitrary arrest for the first time in their history and instituting press censorship. They increased the size of the army and operated a network of police spies. González Flores fled to the United States, where he persuaded President Woodrow Wilson to withhold recognition of the usurper government. Wilson, who was having enough trouble trying to promote democracy in Latin America, was not about to permit it to fail in the one country where it seemed to be working. *Tico* democracy may have had sufficient strength to survive on its own, but Wilson's action compounded Tinoco's problems severely. When the United States entered World War I, and Wilson embarked on his crusade to make the world safe for democracy, Federico Tinoco's days in office were numbered. In San José in May 1919, a mass demonstration by schoolteachers and students led to a clash with the army and police and further discredited Tinoco. The Olympians began to speak out, and émigrés based in Nicaragua prepared for an armed invasion. In August 1919, Tinoco abruptly resigned and departed from the country. Having learned a harsh lesson, the *ticos* — the oligarchy included — quickly restored democratic institutions, but the economic and social problems that had been at the root of the turmoil of these years persisted, and the issues that González Flores had raised continued to demand attention.

These issues especially troubled Jorge Volio, who had been one of the heroes in the resistance against the Tinoco brothers. He had led an unsuccessful uprising against the Tinoco distatorship, and he took refuge in Nicaragua, where he joined other exiles in preparing an armed expedition. Volio, a member of a distinguished Cartago family, had been a Catholic priest until 1915, when his advanced social ideas got him into trouble with the Costa Rican Catholic hierarchy. He had studied at the University of Louvain in Belgium, where he came under the influence of the progressive Cardinal Mercier and the new social doctrines of Pope Leo XIII and of the encyclical *Rerum Novarum*. With his social conscience aroused, he believed that it was a priest's duty to do more than say mass, and he undertook to implement the Christian message of charity, love, and justice. Although he renounced the priesthood, because his combative spirit refused to yield to the church's discipline, he never really doffed his priestly robes. He deplored the lack of ideological content in Costa Rican politics and criticized the oligarchy, which, he charged, "governed for its own benefit, oblivious of the problems of the people" (Barahona, 1971). He wrote that it was "no longer possible to accept the spectacle of a people burdened by written laws while they die of hunger" (Barahona, 1971). Following Tinoco's fall, the adventurous and charismatic Volio founded the Reformist Party in 1923, based upon social Christian philosophy.

The Reformist Party was the first truly social movement in Costa Rican history. Although Volio argued that the party was based upon ideas, and not personalities, his own personality was so overwhelming that the movement never had a chance to acquire an identity of its own. Nonetheless, the movement constituted a challenge to the passive rule of the liberal patriarchs and to the free-wheeling manner of the coffee elites. In addition, the challenge came from within the *conquistador* class itself, since Volio possessed the *sangre*, and it provided yet another precedent for the progressive role the Catholic church would play in the future. The Reformist Party program called for the taxation of incomes; improved public education, including the reopening of the university; a civil service; better wages and working conditions for labor, including the right to organize and bargain collectively; and an end to the monopolistic practices of the coffee oligarchs and foreign enterprises. Volio was one of the first to voice antiimperialistic sentiments, wherein he attacked the United Fruit Company and supported the inalienability of sub-surface wealth. In 1924, Volio presented himself as the Reformist Party's candidate for president.

The election of 1924 was another three-way contest in which no candidate received the required majority. Despite the fact that Volio had said he would not be a party to a deal, because it was not possible to compromise with the status quo, he gave his support to Ricardo Jiménez and accepted the vice presidency in return. Volio's action meant the demise of the Reformist Party and the return of the liberal patriarchy to power. Subsequently, in 1926, Volio tried to overthrow the government, and Jiménez, reluctant to imprison a patriot, sent him abroad for psychiatric care, which his frequent bizarre behavior made credible. For 12 years, from 1924 to 1936, the Olympians ruled Costa Rica again in relative calm, with Don

Ricardo serving twice, but not in consecutive terms, and Don Cleto serving once. They governed honestly and responsibly and administered the laws equitably. Scholars have speculated as to how they managed to dominate affairs for so long, given the fact that they seemed content merely to preserve the gains of the past and were unresponsive to ills outside the legal and political spheres. Some suggest that the closing of the university in 1888 retarded intellectual development and impeded the rise of new leaders that could challenge them. Indeed, Don Cleto and Don Ricardo failed to groom any successor and their strong personalities stifled would-be rivals and convinced the people that they were irreplaceable. In truth, their political longevity may be attributed to the fact that, although popular and liberal, they never constituted a threat to the coffee barons. The Olympians were what the name implied; they managed to maintain the status quo in a society with increasing economic and social injustices, and to do it with honor and good will and without repression. But the deluge was coming.

The worldwide economic depression of 1929 was a sharp blow to *tico* complacency. In 1928, Costa Rica produced 16,526,000 kilos of coffee at 60¢ per kilo. Five years later, the yield reached 24,578,000 kilos, but the price fell to only 27¢ a kilo. Comparing the two crops, Costa Rica produced almost half again as much and earned one-third less. Given the fact that coffee accounted for 70 percent of all exports in 1933, it does not take much imagination to translate these figures into human misery. As González Flores had done earlier, Jiménez attempted to deal with the crisis through fiscal restraints on credit, the amount of money in circulation, and the convertibility of foreign exchange, all of which only increased unemployment. In the end, the government abandoned its laissez-faire policy, and, in 1933, Jiménez intervened directly in the coffee industry in an effort to stabilize prices and regulate production. These measures could not stem the increasing unrest of labor, which provided the opportunity for the rise of the Communist Party.

Some scholars attribute the rise of the Communist Party to the disappearance of the Reformist Party. With no viable alternative to the predominance of the Olympians, *tico* youth supposedly had only Marx and anti-Yankee literature to turn to. Law-school students, such as Manuel Mora Valverde, were attracted to the position of the Civic League, an incipient Marxist group totally opposed to foreign economic interests in Costa Rica, especially to U.S. companies. *Tico* historian Oscar Aguilar Bulgarelli (1969) argues that the Marxist ideas of class struggle and violent revolution "totally ignored" the *tico* idiosyncrasy and resulted in very few followers of Marx in Costa Rica. Nonetheless, the economic crisis of 1929 created desperate times, and Mora, a descendent of the *conqistadores* himself, helped found the Communist Party officially in 1931. The Communist movement did not make a great deal of headway on the Meseta, outside youthful intellectual circles, but conditions on the banana plantations of Limón provided greater opportunities for the movement.

The depression hit the banana zone particularly hard. There, declining production and rising unemployment aggravated an already poor relationship between the United Fruit Company and its workers. Added to this was racial strife between the black workers brought in by the company and unemployed, white Meseta peasants who had migrated to the region in search of work. The white workers complained that the blacks enjoyed a privileged position, because they spoke English and communicated better with the fruit company's North American managers. When, in the midst of all these economic and social problems, the Panama disease (a fungus that destroys the banana bushes) struck the Limón plantations, and United Fruit considered relocating on the Pacific coast, the white workers agitated to prevent the migration of blacks from Limón province. These factors provided the Communists with an opportunity to test their organizing skills. The workers were concentrated; they worked for a single employer; and the United Fruit Company, already a symbol of Yankee imperialism, proved a very convenient and popular target.

In 1933, Communist Party leader Carlos Luis Fallas, a popular novelist and another defector from the *conquistador* class, began organizing the banana workers, allegedly with the help of Sandinistas from Nicaragua. Fallas was particularly successful in convincing white and black workers to unite in a common cause. By the following year, he felt confident enough to lead a strike against the banana company, and he managed to win union recognition and wage guarantees. On the Meseta, troubled leading citizens demanded that Jiménez take action against the strikers, but Don Ricardo refused to act as long as the strikers obeyed the law. "The reality is that the Communists exist," he declared, and admonished the coffee barons about any illegal acts (Rodríguez Vega, 1971). However, when the strike was renewed in August 1934, over charges that the fruit company failed to comply with the labor contract, and violence occurred, Jiménez sent troops to Limón to restore order. Although the Communist Party's success was confined mainly to the banana zone, it decided to present candidates for the presidency and Congress in 1936, under the label of the Workers' and Peasants' Bloc.

By 1936, the coffee barons were disillusioned with the leadership of the liberal patriarchs and sought a firmer hand. They resented their diminished influence, measured by increased taxation, and blamed Don Ricardo's suffrage-extending policies for the growth of the Communist Party. The coffee barons supported the candidacy of León Cortés, Jiménez's minister of development, who ran under Don Ricardo's party label, the National Republican Party, even though Don Ricardo was only lukewarm toward him. But in any event, personalism continued to determine elections. Cortés, although a civilian, enjoyed the title of *caudillo*, and he gave the oligarchy the tougher rule it wanted, revealing paternalism's sharp edges. He harassed the Communist Party and refused to permit Manuel Mora, elected as deputy from San José, to be seated in the national Congress. Besides being stern, Cortés displayed marked pro-Nazi sentiments. German immigrants in Costa Rica had assumed increasing importance; they were coffee entrepreneurs themselves and many had married into the leading families. The names — Rohrmorer, Reimers, Lehmann, Steinvort, Federspiel, Effinger, and Koberg — were among the most prominent in the nation. In addition, by this time, Germany had replaced England as Costa Rica's best customer for coffee. This situation added to the woes of the coffee oligarchy during World War II.

In the meantime, Cortés undertook to perpetuate his rule by handpicking Rafael Angel Calderón Guardia, a mild-mannered pediatrician and the pliable president of the national Congress, as his successor in 1940. Despite continued unemployment, lack of public services, and widespread poverty, compounded by the fact that the population had reached 660,000, Cortés contemplated no changes. Don Ricardo Jiménez was now 80, but many sectors of the population, including peasants, intellectuals, and students, looked to him to challenge the *caudillo*. Jiménez announced his candidacy, only to withdraw in less than three weeks, in the face of overwhelming odds — money and official backing behind Calderón — plus acts of violence committed against his supporters by Cortés's thugs. Oddly enough, given so many pressing issues, the principal factor that induced Jiménez to try again had been his concern over Calderón's close ties to the church, as one of Costa Rica's leading lay Catholics. This had struck a nerve in the old liberal. But more ironic was the fact that Calderón's strong attachment to the church resulted in his being a far different president than Cortés or anyone else had expected.

Calderón Guardia proved to be one of the most dynamic presidents in Costa Rican history and one of the two men responsible for the nature of the Costa Rican state today. Calderón had studied at the University of Louvain, where he, similar to Volio, was influenced by the social doctrines of the Catholic church, as expressed in the papal encyclicals of Leo XIII and Pius XI. When he returned to San José, he established a very successful practice as a pediatrician, leading to the observation that many of the people who voted for him had also been delivered by him. He was elected to Congress more on his reputation as a doctor and doer of charitable works than as a politican, and as president of that body during Cortés's term, he cooperated with the *caudillo* fully. Cortés believed he would be a perfect puppet, but once he achieved the presidency, his concern for the suffering of the poor took over and he cast Cortés aside. Unlike Volio, Calderón encountered a synpathetic church leader in the person of Archbishop Víctor Sanabria Martínez. Sanabria was a remarkable prelate who believed firmly in social Christian doctrine and favored the church's active participation — indeed, obligation — in resolving the economic and social ills of the day. Sanabria encouraged Calderón to undertake a massive program of social reform.

Calderón established the Office of Social Security in 1941, and, the following year, proposed to amend the constitution to include "social guarantees." Calderón's social security program included accident, sickness, disability, old age, and unemployment benefits and called for the creation of hospitals and clinics for the provision of medical and health care. His social guarantees included an eight-hour day, a minimum wage, the right of workers and employers to organize, requirements for safe and healthful working conditions, preferential treatment for Costa Ricans in the job market, provisions for the establishment of cooperatives, and measures fot improved housing. In 1943, he enacted a comprehensive Labor Code, incorporating many of the social guarantees and regulating relations between workers and employers. Calderón also reopened the University of Costa Rica. He had begun the transformation of Costa Rica from a liberal, democratic state to a welfare state.

Predictably, the oligarchs were incensed by his actions. Their anger increased when Costa Rica entered World War II in December 1941, and when Calderón seized the property of a number of aliens. This step offended the oligarchy deeply, because of its intimate ties, through business and marriage, to German and Italian residents. Many of the old families set up dummy companies in their own names, in order to provide a protective cover for the so-called alien properties – a practice that Calderón condemned. In 1942, members of the oligarchy began to plot the overthrow of Calderón and even approached Manuel Mora, seeking his cooperation. Instead, the Communist leader went to Calderón and proposed an alliance. With the Soviet Union a wartime ally, Calderón could respond favorably to such an offer with less criticism. When some of Calderón's own followers objected, showing concern over the reaction of the church, Mora and Sanabria engaged in a public exchange of letters in which Mora announced the dissolution of the Communist Party and the formation of a new party (the Popular Vanguard), which rejected any doctrine in conflict with the church; and Sanabria declared that the new party had "no conflicts of conscience" for Catholics (Ameringer, 1979). Calderón merged his National Republican Party with Mora's Popular Vanguard so as to form the Victory Bloc, attempting to create a patriotic appearance. By 1943, Calderón was governing Costa Rica with the collaboration of the Communists and the Catholic church. Costa Rican politics were becoming intricate and there was some question as to how *tico* democracy might handle the situation.

Affairs became more complex with the appearance of a social democratic movement. The movement originated in 1940 when the Center for the Study of National Problems was formed by a group of recent law-school graduates, who recognized the bankruptcy of the old liberalism and rejected the extremism of the Communists. They were sons and grandsons of the less-favored sons, who wanted to modernize the state and expand the role of government, as a means both of improving the living conditions of Costa Ricans and of providing greater opportunity for themselves. They were influenced by the Aprista doctrine (the movement of Víctor Raúl Haya de la Torre of Peru), which called for social reform, planning, and government intervention in the economy, without sacrificing democracy. They had opposed Calderón in 1940 as being only more of the same, finding out too late that he was different. However, even then, the young men of the Center (Centristas), weighed down by the old anticlerical barnacles, could not support his prochurch position, and criticized him when he readmitted the Jesuits and reintroduced religious instruction in the schools. Calderón's wooing of Mora alienated them also, particularly as they perceived authoritarian tendencies on the part of Calderón himself and believed that he tolerated acts of violence by the comrades. In the election of 1944, faced with the choice of Calderón's puppet, Teodoro Picado, or the old *caudillo*, León Cortés, they supported the latter on the basis that at least he was a democrat, although they made it clear they did not wish to abandon the social reforms. Their collective conscience was eased a bit by the presence, in the Cortés camp, of a reformist element led by José Figueres.

Figueres, the other of the creators of the modern Costa Rican state, burst upon the political scene in 1942, when he was 35 years old. Until that time, he had operated a *finca* in a hard-to-reach area just beyond the Meseta, where he achieved a modest reputation for his industry, initiative, and progressive, though paternalistic, treatment of his workers. In July 1942, an Axis submarine torpedoed a United Fruit Company vessel in Limón harbor, touching off a riot in San José, in which mobs sacked and looted the businesses and properties of Germans and Italians in the city. Deploring such waste and violence, Figures purchased radio time to denounce the Calderón government. He criticized the government for failing to restrain the mob and suggested, in fact, that Calderón and the Communists actually perpetrated the riot. Calderón immediately arrested Figueres and expelled him from the country. He accused Figueres of being a Nazi and produced documents linking Figueres to a company sheltering the properties of Federico Reimers, a longtime German resident of Costa Rica. There was little to suggest that Figueres was a Nazi, and most people regarded the charge as false. In time, Calderón's popularity declined, Figueres emerged as a hero for having been the first to speak out against him. When Figueres returned to San José from his exile in Mexico, following the election of 1944, a huge crowd came to the airport to greet him.

In March 1945, Figueres, identified as a reform-minded member of Cortés's Democratic Party, and the Centristas joined forces to form the Social Democratic Party. The party was dedicated to economic and social reform within a democratic context, and, although very small, hoped to participate in an opposition coalition in the 1948 election. By this time, Calderón's image as a strongman had grown, particularly since there had been incidents of violence and fraud in the 1944 election. Calderón is a much-misunderstood leader. The consensus is that he was a reformer, not a revolutionary, and that he may be described best as a populist; Mora described him as an idealist and a romantic. Nonetheless, with the coming of the cold war, his continued link with the Communists provided convenient fodder for his political opponents and made him vulnerable to the charge of being a dictator. His intention to run again for the presidency in 1948 proved a rallying point for all his opponents, who, although representing contradictory viewpoints, felt in common a distaste for Calderón and a fierce anticommunism. The opposition formed a coalition made up of the coffee barons, who wanted to eliminate the social guarantees; the candidate, Otilio Ulate, a newspaper publisher, who longed for the good old days of the liberal patriarchy; the Social Democrats, who wanted reform and democracy; and Figueres, who wanted revenge.

Figueres was not as sanguine as the others, who felt that Calderón would permit a free election. While they were engaged in an electoral campaign, Figueres took steps to prepare for armed action, just in case. Figueres had been born in Costa Rica only a few months after his parents had arrived there from Barcelona, and he referred to himself as a Catalán. Ulate observed that Figueres possessed a mentality alien to the *tico* idiosyncrasy and was not surprised that he was less inclined to resolve matters *a la tica*. While Figueres had been in exile in Mexico, he came into contact with exiles from numerous other Central American and Caribbean states, and they discussed the common problem of dictatorship in the region. After World War II, various exile groups (erroneously lumped together under the term Caribbean Legion) developed plans for armed expeditions against the dictators of the Caribbean — especially Rafael Trujillo of the Dominican Republic and Anastasio Somoza of Nicaragua — with the help of the governments of Cuba and Guatemala. In December 1947, Figueres traveled to Guatemala and negotiated the Pact of the Caribbean, in which, in return for arms and other military assistance, if necessary, for overthrowing Calderón, he pledged to help the exile groups in operations against Nicaragua, the Dominican Republic, and other dictatorships in the Caribbean zone. Although no other *tico* leaders were privy to this scheme, it turned out that Figueres's way was necessary to get rid of Calderón.

The election of 1948 was a bitter and hard-fought campaign, marred by incidents of violence on both sides. When the ballots were counted, it appeared that Ulate had won, but Calderón accused the opposition of fraud and ballot stuffing and used his control of the Congress to nullify the election. While most of the opposition appeared paralyzed by this maneuver, Figueres withdrew to his *finca* in the mountains to the south and called upon his Caribbean allies to fulfill their pledge. Within hours after Figueres raised the cry of revolt on March 11, his allies airlifted two planeloads of arms from Guatemala, and experienced military chieftains arrived to train his volunteer army. Despite the charges that Calderón was a dictator, Costa Rica lacked an army to meet this challenge, and most of the fighting was done by the Communists, who relied upon the organized workers from the banana regions. The Costa Rican civil war lasted six weeks, and cost 2,000 lives before Figueres's triumphant forces entered San José on April 24, 1948.

The outside world did not know what to make of the conflict. It seemed so out of character with the reputation of Costa Rica. Owing to the diverse elements fighting on each side, the observers who called the movement revolutionary were matched by those who called it reactionary. In truth, the civil war of 1948 confirmed the rise of a number of transitional forces in Costa Rica since the early 1940s and marked the political decline of the oligarchy. The oligarchy backed the struggle in order to put Ulate in the presidency, but the armed rebels had no intention of restoring the oligarchs to power, nor of scrapping the reforms of Calderón. In the end, the so-called eight years of Calderón were as much a part of the Costa Rican revolution as was the civil war of 1948. The forces under Figueres restored *tico* democray, but set in motion a process that entirely recast the structure and role of government. They fought to defend Ulate's right to the presidency, but they had their own ideas and they had the guns, so by the time he got the chance to govern, they presented him with a fait accompli.

Before Figueres turned over the government to Ulate, he and his Social Democratic followers governed provisionally for 18 months, in order to establish what Figueres − Don Pepe − called the Second Republic. The provisional junta nationalized the banks and levied a 10 percent across-the-board tax on assets valued at more than ₡50,000. The junta held elections for a Constituent Assembly and oversaw the drafting of a new constitution. Although the constitution of 1949 was not everything that Figueres and the junta wanted, it provided the basis for the creation of a new Costa Rican state. It provided especially for the creation of autonomous agencies − that is, state agencies to guide, regulate, or perform virtually every task in the social and economic spheres. At the same time, while the constitution permitted an enlarged role for government and legalized the extension of the public sector, it attempted to decentralize power within the national government, by curtailing the authority of the presidency. Moreover, it created the Supreme Electoral Tribunal, which assured the freest and fairest electoral machinery of any country in the world. It also extended suffrage to women. The constitution was only an instrument; how it was used depended upon the leadership and ingenuity of Don Pepe and his followers. In time, they used it very well, remaking the Costa Rican state to fulfill their aims.

After transferring the presidency to Ulate in 1949, Figueres won election to the office in his own right, by an overwhelming majority, in 1953. In the meantime, Don Pepe and the former Social Democrats founded the National Liberation Party (PLN) in 1951. A majority of the founders of the PLN were descendants of the *conquistadores*, which meant a further differentiation of this class, but which also helped it to maintain the remarkable cohesiveness of *tico* society. The PLN was the first political party worthy of the name in Costa Rican history. It had a defined political program, with a permanent organization and structure that gave it a life of its own. The party embraced representative democracy and called for the broadest possible action of government, in order to provide for social justice and economic opportunity, without excluding the right of private property. It followed the concepts of a mixed economy and a multi-class society, although it gave priority to the authority of the state in seeking the greatest good for the greatest number. Despite the overriding goal of the Liberacionistas for a permanent, ideological party, the ever-present personalism in *tico* politics remained a factor, and all the more so because of the charisma of Don Pepe.

Figueres adhered to, and, in fact, inspired much of the philosophy of the PLN, but he also left the mark of his own peculiar ideas upon the Costa Rican order in the years of his two presidencies, 1953-58 and 1970-74. Figueres spent four years of his youth, 1924-28, in the United States, where he acquired a great deal of respect for North American institutions, and later he was deeply influenced by the programs of the New Deal during the Great Depression. As a *finquero* (planter), Figueres demonstrated a strong commitment to the idea that the success of his enterprise was intimately linked to the improvement and well-being of his workers. Figueres believed that production and the just distribution of its fruits were more important than the ownership of the means of production. He abhorred the class struggle, because he felt that class harmony was essential for full production, and he longed for the creation of one vast middle class. For this reason, he promoted education and technical training, so that there might be full utilization of human resources. These ideas were merged with the more doctrinaire programs of the PLN and resulted in the structure of the Costa Rican state as it is today.

During Figueres's presidencies, the function of the state gradually expanded. In addition to banking and social security, Figueres and other PLN presidents (Francisco Orlich, in 1962-66; and Daniel Oduber, in 1974-78) created autonomous institutions to deal with such matters as insurance, electrical energy, housing, national planning, agrarian reform, tourism, telecommunications, and transportation. By 1980, the number of government agencies had swelled to 182, and the bureaucracy and public sector employed almost one-fifth of the entire work force. Moreover, the welfare state the PLN created was not dismantled during the times that its leaders did not occupy the president's chair. *Tico* democracy continued to operate during this process of change. In fact, from the time that Figueres was first elected president in 1953 and until the present, on only one occasion (1974) did the PLN succeed itself in office. Those who had built the new Costa Rican state since 1948 found both strength and weakness in *tico* democracy. Defeats in elections have interrupted the progress of their programs, but they transformed society without violating individual freedom, and what they have accomplished rests firmly upon the legitimacy of the political process. Despite criticisms that they have not gone far enough — since there is still serious poverty, and the lands of the coffee barons remain untouched — the Liberacionistas are confident that representative democracy is the most effective vehicle for the attainment of economic and social progress. The safeguards in the constitution against excessive presidential power and centralized control, in a society where the state is now expected to provide all the answers, cause problems, but this is the uniqueness and dilemma of *tico* democracy. Today, *tico* democracy both cares for and frustrates the needs of the people.

3

THE COSTA RICAN STATE:
MACHINERY AND POLICY

The constitution of 1949 is the fundamental law of Costa Rica. It provides for a unitary republic and, as such, determines the rights, duties, and guarantees of all citizens and the relationships among every branch and level of government. It is the guarantor of the proper functioning of the political and legal processes and the basis for the extensive functioning of the state today in the cultural, social, and economic spheres. Unlike the constitutions of many Latin American states, which are merely visionary museum pieces, the Costa Rican Constitution of 1949 is built upon a firm foundation of historical experience and *tico* reality.

Because the constitution was written in the aftermath of the civil war of 1948, during the period of rule by the so-called founding junta, one might conclude that it reflected the viewpoint of the victors in the war and that it was imposed upon the country. Such was not the case. Although the delegates to the Constituent Assembly were elected under the authority of the junta, José Figueres and the Social Democrats making up the junta maintained such impartiality and restraint that only a handful of their partisans actually won seats. The situation was compounded by the fact that the Social Democratic Party was small and inexperienced, and that its most prominent members, then serving on the junta, did not consider it appropriate to stand for election. Almost to the point of naiveté, they left the field open to the traditional and conservative elements of the coalition that were opposed to Rafael Calderón, particularly the followers of President-elect Otilio Ulate. The Constituent Assembly rejected out of hand a draft constitution prepared by the junta, and used the constitution of 1871 as its model. Figueres exerted pressure by threatening to resign and precipitate a crisis, but such actions do not alter the fact that the 1949 constitution was drafted by a body beyond his direct control and influence. The maneuvers of Figueres cannot be ignored, but a large share of the credit for key elements and important changes in the basic law of Costa Rica belongs to the small band of Social Democrats in the Assembly, who prevailed by persuasiveness and force of reason. The document owes its existence to debate and compromise, and not to the domination of a single group.

There were some aspects of the new constitution upon which the Social Democrats and the Ulatistas could agree. These points of agreement responded to the experience of the eight years of Calderón's rule and to the action of nullifying the election of 1948. They resulted in measures to weaken the presidency, including a provision to preserve the principle of the alternation of those in power, in order to prevent the rise, ever again, of a strongman; and the creation of a virtual fourth branch of government, the Supreme Electoral Tribunal, in order to establish the absolute freedom and integrity of elections. The constitution, as drafted in 1949, also outlawed the Communist Party. Most of the delegates agreed upon the preservation of individual and political rights and guarantees, and upon the state's having the principal responsibility for education and cultural advancement. Where the Social Democrats parted company from the majority and left their imprint may be found in the maintenance of Calderón's social guarantees, the extension of suffrage to women, the establishment of the civil service, and the creation of the autonomous institutions of government. Within the constitution, the Social Democrats embodied provisions and machinery that could be used to undertake a broader distribution of wealth, and under which the state might assume the major role in the economy, thereby extending the public sector into any area where the private sector had either failed to take the initiative or was serving narrow interests. In creating this structure, the Social Democrats sought to protect it from the vagaries of politics, so the system of checks and balances and the decentralization of power built into the constitution, which later haunted them, were not the handiwork of the traditional or conservative elements alone. This strange combination of enlarged responsibility and dispersed authority may be understood best by examining the executive branch.

The constitution of 1949 created a significantly weakened office of the presidency and distributed power widely within the executive branch itself. The president is elected popularly for a four-year term and originally could not succeed himself until eight years had elapsed. In 1969, the Legislative Assembly (Congress) amended the constitution to limit future presidents to a single term of office, with no opportunity ever to serve again. This means that every president is a lame duck, with the prospect, depending upon his will and personality, of either being ignored or being able to act boldly and above politics. In reviewing the constitutional limitations upon the presidency, one should not overlook the aspect of personality, because the Costa Rican presidency is similar to the U.S. presidency in that the office, within prescribed limits, is what the incumbent makes of it. The president may appoint and remove ministers of government, who oversee the functions of their respective departments and make up the Council of Government; but this same power at levels below minister, though technically his, is subject to civil-service regulations. The president may issue decrees, which have the force of law, although they may not be in conflict with existing laws. This is a power that presidents have used increasingly in recent times, probably as a result of frustrations experienced in the decades of the fifties and sixties, and it is having some effect upon the nature of the presidency. In times of emergency, the president may suspend guarantees, but such an action is subject to a two-thirds approval of the Legislative Assembly. If the Assembly is not in session at the time, the president's action is an automatic call for an extraordinary session, and the Assembly must meet within 48 hours to sanction the act. The president may initiate legislation through an appropriate minister (which thus gives a semi-parliamentary form to the Costa Rican system), but this is a shared power, in that the president acts jointly with the minister in question. The president has a veto power over legislation, but the Assembly may override a veto by means of a two-thirds vote. Power in all other matters, including the preparation of the budget, the use of military force in war and peace,the conduct of foreign relations, and the negotiation of treaties, is subject to the approval of the Legislative Assembly. The president is specifically enjoined from any act that may compromise the freedom, independence, or territorial integrity of the republic and from any measure that may impede or obstruct, directly or indirectly, the presidential succession or the free exercise of the suffrage. Finally, the distrust of presidential power is extended to encompass the functions of the executive branch itself.

The constitution of 1949 embraces a concept of a plural executive, albeit loosely, in which the president shares power with the Council of Government. Although the president may issue decrees, as mentioned, none are valid without the endorsement of the appropriate minister, and any legislation submitted to the Legislative Assembly by the executive branch must be presented by the minister under whose jurisdiction the measure falls. True, the president may appoint and remove his ministers at will, but such a system, particularly where individual freedoms are effectively exercised, requires cooperation, and not a heavy hand, in order to be credible. Ministers, moreover, must submit an annual report to the Legislative Assembly and are subject to interpellation and censure by that body. In other matters, such as calling upon the Legislative Assembly to declare a state of national emergency, or the appointment of directors of the autonomous institutions, the full Council of Government must approve. The president acts alone, therefore, in only some functions; in all others, he either acts jointly with a specific minister or in concert with the Council of Government. The power of the president over numerous other functions normally associated with the executive branch, particularly the economic and social responsibilities established by the constitution of 1949, is even more limited.

In the drafting of the constitution of 1949, the Social Democrats considered their principal achievement to be the creation of the autonomous institutions. These are institutions established to perform social and cultural services for the public, to regulate and control social and economic activity in the private sector, and to carry out directly certain economic functions – specifically, in the areas of banking, public utilities, and development. When the constitution was drafted, there already existed the Office of Social Security, the nationalized banking system, the National Liquor Factory, and the state-owned Pacific Electric Railway, all of which served as models for the institution concept. The Social Democrats had many more such institutions in mind for the expansion of the public sector and they were anxious to protect their permanence and independence, not only in the area of personnel, but in policy as well. They did not want their activities or their existence to be altered by the possible changes in political power every four years. They indeed intended to institutionalize social reform and the principle of state intervention in, and direction of, the economy. Rodrigo Facio, the man most responsible for this concept, looked upon the problem as a technical one, in which the techniques of a planned economy could be built into the system, without altering the liberal, democratic process. He merged liberal and socialist ideas, with the result that the constitution of 1949 gives the state the responsibility for the economic and social well-being of all the people and makes possible the creation of the machinery for carrying out the task, but separates that machinery (the autonomous institutions) from the authority of those responsible for overall policy making and the conduct of government. Facio did not foresee that there would ever be a conflict between the two, except where there might be an administration hostile to the concept itself, but even friendly administrations have encountered serious problems in the areas of general policy and specific action.

The autonomous institutions are truly autonomous. The president, with the approval of the Council of Government, may appoint the institution directors and, with the approval of the Legislative Assembly, may remove them, but he has no direct power of appointment or removal of officials or personnel further down the line. Although the autonomous institutions are not part of the civil-service system, they have their own system of personnel selection and retention, which protects them from partisan politics. Although some are dependent upon the budgetary process for funds, specific ones have, mandated by law, a certain percentage of the national budget, such as the University of Cost Rica (UCR); and others are profit making, such as the National Insurance Institute (INS). In all cases, they are accountable for their expenditures solely to the Office of the Comptroller General of the republic, which is itself an independent entity. In the conduct of their daily operations, the directors and the governing boards of the autonomous institutions may act in total independence of presidential authority and have even assumed a quasi-legislative function through the establishment of procedures and rules and regulations. The constitution established the principle of governmental action in economic and social affairs, but created a highly decentralized system. The people in a remote area, for example, may petition the central government for safe drinking water, but it is the Costa Rican Institute of Aqueducts and Sewers (ICAA) that determines if and when they get it.

Despite this decentralization and independence among the autonomous institutions, the PLN (National Liberation) governments created scores of them as their means of transforming and developing Costa Rican society. By 1978, according to the Office of National Planning and Economic Policy (OFIPLAN), the number of autonomous institutions had risen to 182, of which 96 had been created since 1950, and, of those, 76 were established after 1960. The central government assumed responsibility for everything from banking and housing to oil refining and the care of alcoholics. The following list of the principal institutions, state agencies, and government ministries provides an idea of the nature and extent of the Costa Rican executive branch. Keep in mind that, for the most part, outside of the ministries, the president's direct control over these entities is greatly curtailed.

BCCR (Banco Central de Costa Rica) Central Bank of Costa Rica
BPDC (Banco Popular y de Desarrollo Comunal) Popular and Community Development Bank
CCSS (Caja Costarricense de Seguro Social) Costa Rican Office of Social Security
CEN (Consejo Económico Nacional) National Economic Council
CIN (Consejo Industrial Nacional) National Industrial Council
CIPIA (Comité Interinstitucional de Pequeña Industria y Artesanía) Interinstitutional Committee of Small Industry and Crafts
CNP (Consejo Nacional de Producción) National Council of Production
CODESA (Corporación Costarricense de Desarrollo, S.A.) Costa Rican Development Corporation

CONAI (Comisión Nacional de Asuntos Indígenas) National Commission for Indian Affairs

CONICIT (Consejo Nacional de Investigaciones Científicas y Tecnológicas) National Council for Scientific and Technological Research

DGAF (Dirección General de Asignaciones Familiares) General Administration of Family Allotments

DINADECO (Dirección Nacional de Desarrollo de la Comunidad) National Administration for Community Development

FECOSA (Ferrocarriles de Costa Rica, S.A.) Costa Rica Railways

ICAA (Instituto Costarricense de Acueductos y Alcantarillados) Costa Rican Institute of Aqueducts and Sewers

ICE (Instituto Costarricense de Electricidad) Costa Rican Institute of Electricity

ICT (Instituto Costarricense de Turismo) Costa Rican Institute of Tourism

IFAM (Instituto de Fomento y Asesoría Municipal) Costa Rican Institute for Municipal Development and Consultation

IMAS (Instituto Mixto de Ayuda Social) Combined Institute of Social Assistance

INA (Instituto Nacional de Aprendizaje) National Institute of Vocational Training

INCOP (Instituto Costarricense de Puertos del Pacífico) Costa Rican Institute of Pacific Coast Ports

INFOCOOP (Instituto Costarricense de Fomento Cooperativo) Costa Rican Institute of Cooperative Development

INS (Instituto Nacional de Seguros) National Insurance Institute

INSA (Instituto Nacional sobre Alcoholismo) National Institute on Alcoholism

INVU (Instituto Nacional de Vivienda y Urbanismo) National Institute of Housing and Urban Development

ITCO (Instituto de Tierras y Colonización) Institute of Lands and Colonization (for agrarian reform)

JAPDEVA (Junta Administrativa Portuaria de la Vertiente Atlántica) Administrative Port Authority of the Atlantic Coast (for Limón development)

LACSA (Líneas Aéreas Costarricenses, S.A.) Costa Rican Airlines

MAG (Ministerio de Agricultura y Ganadería) Ministry of Agriculture and Stockraising

MCJD (Ministerio de Cultura, Juventud y Deportes) Ministry of Culture, Youth, and Sports

MEIC (Ministerio de Economia, Industria y Comercio) Ministry of Economy, Industry, and Trade

MEP (Ministerio de Educación Pública) Ministry of Public Education

MH (Ministerio de Hacienda) Ministry of the Treasury

MJ (Ministerio de Justica) Ministry of Justice

MOPT (Ministerio de Obras Públicas y Transportes) Ministry of Public Works and Transportation

MP (Ministerio de la Presidencia) Ministry of the Presidency

MREC (Ministerio de Relaciones Exteriores y Culto) Ministry of Foreign Relations and Religion

MS (Ministerio de Salud) Ministry of Health

MSP (Ministerio de Seguridad Pública) Ministry of Public Security

MTSS (Ministerio de Trabajo y Seguridad Social) Ministry of Labor and Social Security

OFICAFE (Oficina del Café) National Coffee Office

OFIPLAN (Oficina de Planificación Nacional y Política Económica) Office of National Planning and Economic Policy

OSN (Orquesta Sinfónica Nacional) National Symphonic Orchestra

RECOPE (Refinadora Costarricense de Petróleo) Costa Rican Petroleum Refinery

SBN (Sistema Bancario Nacional) National Banking System

SPN (Servicio de Parques Nacionales) National Parks Service

UCR (Universidad de Costa Rica) University of Costa Rica

UNA (Universidad Nacional) National University (Heredia)

UNED (Universidad Estatal a Distancia) State University Without Walls

The autonomous institutions and state enterprises listed above were created in piecemeal fashion, one at a time, in order to meet a specific need. Aside from the overall philosophy guiding their creation, the existing institutions represented improvisation rather than central planning. In recent times, presidents have attempted to coordinate the activities of these agencies through the creation of broad policy or planning organizations, such as OFIPLAN and DINADECO (the National Community Development Administration), and have had some success in using such devices as budgetary allocations and political rewards. In 1974, President

Daniel Oduber created the position of executive president, which presides over the board of directors of each autonomous institution or state enterprise and acts as liaison between a particular agency and the Council of Government, but the directors still exercise great freedom in administering their little kingdoms. In fact, many set policy and assume responsibilities beyond the original intent of their agency. For example, in 1949, Figueres created the National Council of Production (CNP), which aims to stabilize agricultural prices and stimulate production by acting as an intermediary between farmer and consumer. It built grain elevators, silos, and cold-storage facilities to hold agricultural commodities and provide for orderly, year-round marketing; but eventually it established food-processing plants and even retail outlets, competing with the private sector it was supposed to stimulate. Similar complaints have been made against the Costa Rican Refining Corporation (RECOPE) and the Costa Rican Development Corporation (CODESA). These actions of the directors, and the actions of the Costa Rican government itself in creating new autonomous institutions, have resulted, of course, in a huge bureaucracy.

According to OFIPLAN, the public sector employed 127,762 persons in 1978, or 18.6 percent of the total work force. Some insist the number is greater, reaching almost one-third of all persons employed. Be that as it may, from a percentage standpoint, Costa Rica has one of the largest bureaucracies in the world. There has been a great deal of criticism about the size of the bureaucracy — demonstrated by the increased cost of government, going from ₡827million in 1950 to ₡8 billion in 1980 — but there is also substantial support for the bureaucracy among knowledgeable Costa Ricans. In 1977, under President Oduber, the presidential Office of Information distributed a questionnaire requesting a number of leading citizens, those with distinct political viewpoints and party affiliations, to comment upon the state bureaucracy. Notwithstanding differences of opinion concerning the effectiveness and efficiency of the bureaucracy and the appropriateness of the functions assumed by the state, the respondents expressed little criticism about the size of the bureaucracy per se, believing that it reflected the growth of the population in general (which in the early seventies was showing a phenomenal 3.7 percent annual growth rate before it slowed a bit toward the end of the decade). They indicated that the requirements of education alóne in handling the demographic explosion might justify the expansion. The problems of the bureaucracy are discussed later in connection with the general problems of *tico* democracy, but it is appropriate here to consider the status of public employees within the state apparatus, particularly with reference to recruitment and job security.

The constitution of 1949 created the civil-service system. The system protects public employees in the ministries and related government agencies (referred to herein as employees of the central government), but not in the autonomous institutions and state enterprises, which have independent personnel policies. The employees of the central government (including teachers within the Ministry of Public Education) are selected on the basis of personal qualifications and competitive examinations and may not be dismissed on the grounds of political views or political-party affiliation. Samuel Stone (1975) and others insist that, even though one must submit to a written examination, party affiliation, personal contacts, and family ties enter into the final selection. The fact that the members of the *conquistador* class, for example, are the best-educated and the best-connected people must be taken into account. However, the days of the wholesale firing of the bureaucracy that followed a change in the political party in power are gone from Costa Rica. In fact, it is very difficult to remove a public employee, which thus causes complaints that the pendulum has swung too far in the direction of job security and has led to immobility and in-efficiency. Nonetheless, public employees are protected against the spoils system, unlike virtually any other government in Latin America, and certainly in Central America.

The civil-service system maintains a uniform salary schedule for all employees under its jurisdiction. In addition to being the most secure, public employees are among the highest-paid workers in Costa Rica. Promotions are generally given on the basis of seniority, creating the additional charge that the system rewards incompetence, if one can remain on the job long enough. Specialists in public administration point out that the civil service in Costa Rica lacks a true merit and career-development system, wherein good work and high quality are the basis for advancement. Interestingly, one group of public employees of the central government that is not protected by civil service, much less having any sort of career-development program, is the 4,000-man Civil Guard within the Ministry of Public Security. It is poorly trained and poorly paid, and there is a turnover rate of from 50 to 90 percent when a new administration comes to power. This exception may be explained by the general fear of militarism on the part of Costa Rican society. *Ticos* do not wish to promote a professional cadre, which could result from better training, higher pay, and greater job security. The largest group of public employees — that of the autonomous institutions — which numbers six times those of the central government, is also outside the civil-service system.

Although the employees of the autonomous institutions are not part of the civil-service system, they are recruited in the same manner and enjoy the same guarantees as those within it. Each autonomous institution has its own personnel system, but must select employees through competitive examinations and may not dismiss anyone without just cause and a proper hearing, and then advance notification and severance pay. Many of the same criticisms, with reference to recruitment, made against agencies of the central government apply to the autonomous institutions, but here, too, the spoils system is a thing of the past. In recent years, proposals have been made for the creation of an integrated, uniform civil-service system for all public-sector employees, but the directors of the autonomous institutions have resisted. Their major defense is the principle of decentralization. They argue that presidents could use the reform as a back door to acquiring control of their agencies. Actually, a change of this nature seems appropriate. Although autonomous institutions must follow standard practices in hiring and firing, there is no uniform salary schedule among them, which results in the raiding of the personnel of poor agencies by affluent ones (such as the ICE or INS). This has the effect of lowering morale and standards within many agencies of the government and leads to labor strife. In addition to being the best-paid and the most secure workers in Costa Rica, public employees are also the best organized.

Organized labor is not strong in Costa Rican society, but among the unions that do exist, the strongest are those of the employees in the public sector. These include the principal teachers' union (ANDE, the National Association of Educators) and the National Association of Public Employees (ANEP). The problems related to these unions, particularly strikes by public employees, will be discussed elsewhere, but it is important to note that their actions have increased the cost of government and have fortified the opponents of the welfare state. When the teachers and other public employees (including doctors and nurses) go out on strike, not only is the public inconvenienced, but significant elements of government cease to function. As public employees take a larger bite out of the budget, they leave less for attending to the purposes they are supposed to serve. Costa Rican presidents have been thwarted in efforts to make reforms because of the decentralized nature of the executive branch. In their distrust of presidential power, the makers of the constitution of 1949 greatly weakened the presidency, but fear of the rise of a strongman is not the sole explanation. The Social Democrats in the 1949 Constituent Assembly, in order to assure the permanence of their reforms and to make them immune to partisan politics, are largely responsible for the dispersal of power within the Costa Rican government. Indeed, although the constitution of 1949 gives greater power to the Legislative Assembly, the legislative branch is effectively checked, particularly against intrusions upon the functions of the autonomous institutions.

The Legislative Assembly is the strongest branch of government in Costa Rica. It is also the most democratic and representative institution. The Legislative Assembly makes and repeals all laws, and its approval is necessary for many actions of the president and the Council of Government, such as the suspension of civil guarantees, the contracting of foreign loans, and the negotiation of international treaties. The Legislative Assembly is a unicameral body consisting of 57 deputies, who are elected for four-year terms and are not immediately eligible for reelection. Deputies are elected according to their position on the party slate in each province. The percentage of votes each party receives in the province determines how many of its candidates, beginning at the top of the list, will go to the Assembly. Although the people do not vote directly for a particular candidate, *ticos* consider the system democratic in that it allows for minority representation. The constitution makers retained the single-chamber legislative body (a feature of the 1871 constitution) because they looked upon the concept of an upper house, or a senate, as elitist and, consequently, less democratic. The constitution of 1949 originally gave the Assembly 45 seats, or one deputy for each 30,000 persons, with a provision for expansion, but, with the tremendous growth of the Costa Rican population after 1950, the lawmakers amended the constitution in 1961 and fixed the number of seats permanently at 57. This requires a periodic reapportioning of seats among the provinces that reflects population changes. Overall, members of the Legislative Assembly are quite young, since deputies need only be 21 years of age, and because of the proscription against successive terms. Very many of the deputies are members of rural-elite families or young lawyers, who use their term to find a position in the central government or to establish business contacts. Deputies enjoy immunity in all their public statements and against imprisonment for any cause. However, in criminal matters the Legislative Assembly may vote to suspend them. Although political dynamics, the manner of deputy selection, and personal ambition may have a bearing upon an individual deputy's behavior, taken collectively, the Costa Rican Congress is no tool of the president, no matter how forceful or resourceful he may be.

The Legislative Assembly is the supreme law-making body of the republic. Bills or resolutions may be initiated by an individual deputy or by an appropriate minister of government. These measures are referred to relevant committees for study and, following their report back to the Assembly, go through three separate readings or debates before final action is taken. This procedure can be very time consuming, because each deputy is entitled to speak for as long as 30 minutes during each debate. Under the constitution, the Assembly is in session for six months of the year, but owing to its procedures and heavy workload, the Assembly is in almost continuous session. The convoking of special sessions to deal with a specific issue is one power the president has over the Assembly, but few deputies object to this, because they are paid on a daily basis, at a fairly high rate, during the time the Assembly is in extraordinary session. Considering the variety of issues it must confront, its relatively small size, and the fact that many of its members lack experience, it is surprising that the Assembly accomplishes as much as it does. Moreover, its activities are closely monitored by the public at large, through broad coverage in the daily press and by means of live radio broadcasts of all sessions. Legislative sessions are frequently accompanied by raucous behavior on the part of packed galleries. *Ticos* are anything but apathetic.

However, the power of the Legislative Assembly is not confined to law-making alone. The legislative branch effectively checks the executive branch in a number of ways. Ministers of government must submit an annual report to the Legislative Assembly and may be summoned to appear before it or any of its committees at any time. The Legislative Assembly is empowered to conduct an investigation of any of the ministers or ministries and to require their subordinates (any citizen, for that matter) to testify. In its investigations, it has unrestricted access to records and documents. If warranted, the Assembly may censure a minister, but it does not have the power to remove the minister. Its power in this regard is moral, but it may result in a resignation. However, the Legislative Assembly may impeach a president or minister of government on grounds specifically stated in the constitution. The president has the power to veto a measure, but he must act within ten days (there is no pocket veto), and the Assembly may override his veto by a vote of two-thirds of the total membership. The approval of the Legislative Assembly is necessary for any traveling that the president wishes to do abroad. The power of the Legislative Assembly is, therefore, quite extensive, although it has lost the jurisdiction it once had over elections and the exercise of the suffrage. The makers of the constitution of 1949 had a distrust of the Congress because of its action nullifying the presidential election of 1948, and they decided to form a new branch of government responsible for the electoral process.

Toward this end, the constitution of 1949 created the Supreme Electoral Tribunal, which has absolute authority in all matters dealing with the exercise of the suffrage, the conduct of elections, and the succession of office. The Supreme Electoral Tribunal is solely responsible for the registration of voters, the issuance of voter-identification cards (*cédulas*), the management of the polls, the composition of electoral boards, the monitoring of political campaigns to ensure compliance with electoral laws, the counting of ballots, and the announcement of election results. The Tribunal alone proclaims the winners of elections, without an opportunity given for appeal. In performing its functions, the Tribunal has at its disposal the police and security forces of the republic, in order to assure the honesty and integrity of elections and the orderly succession of the presidency. The Tribunal is made up of three magistrates and six alternatives who are appointed for six-year terms by the Supreme Court of Justice and who have the possibility of reelection. The appointment of the magistrates and alternatives by the Supreme Court is the only tie that the Tribunal has with any of the other branches of government. In all matters under its authority, it is autonomous and independent, constituting, in effect, a fourth branch of government.

The Tribunal is composed of two departments: the Civil Register, and the Electoral Department. The Civil Register is responsible for preparing and maintaining the lists of registered voters for each polling place and and for issuing voter identification cards, bearing the holder's photograph. In order to facilitate its work, it is responsible for the registration of births, deaths, marriages, and acts of naturalization. As such, it provides a broader service for the nation as an office of vital records and statistics. Because of this control, the Supreme Electoral Tribunal has all but eradicated the incidence of fraud in Costa Rican elections. Costa Rica's reputation for fairness and honesty in elections is one of the highest in the world. The Electoral Department is responsible for the mechanical apparatus of elections and for enforcing the electoral laws. It sees to it that fair campaign practices are followed and that government officials, including the president, maintain absolute impartiality in electoral campaigns. Some presidents have argued that there is a distinction between impartiality and neutrality, but the rulings of the Supreme Electoral Tribunal, with reference to complaints, have been assiduously obeyed. The performance of the Tribunal has been exemplary, and few question its integrity and independence. Only the matter of campaign finances has aroused controversy, and this involves the system, not the conduct of the magistrates.

Costa Rica provides for public financing of political campaigns. In order to overcome the problem of corruption and curb inordinate influence by large contributors, the Supreme Electoral Tribunal pays the campaign debts of political parties, in accordance with the percentage of votes they receive, providing they receive at least 10 percent of the vote. As a result, the National Liberation Party, the best-organized Costa Rican political party, does not rely upon individual contributors for its campaigns. The complaint against the system is the obvious one: that it favors the major, established parties and makes it difficult for new parties to enter the field.

This objection has grown since 1971, when the law was changed to provide prior financing of political campaigns, based upon performance in the immediately preceding election. This procedure contributes to the independence and stability of major political parties and may even promote a two-party system, but minor parties look upon it as undemocratic. It may be noted, however, that there are no limitations upon private contributions, there are no disclosure laws, and public employees may not be dunned. Nonetheless, no one has complained about the Tribunal's honesty in disbursing these funds.

The respect the Supreme Electoral Tribunal enjoys for its integrity and competence is shared by the highest body of judges in the traditional third branch of the government, the judiciary. The constitution of 1949 gave the Supreme Court of Justice broad powers and functions and absolute independence. The members of the Constituent Assembly of 1949, who distrusted the executive and legislative branches, had no misgivings toward the judicial branch. They admired the manner in which the judiciary had conducted itself in Costa Rican history and they undertook to preserve and extend its power under the new constitution. The constitution specifically empowers the Supreme Court to determine the constitutionality of laws (judicial review) and authorizes it to conduct trials in the matter of impeachment. It sits as the court of appeal in all cases involving the free exercise of individual and civil rights and has proved a strong defender of those rights. The Supreme Court is made up of 17 justices elected by the Legislative Assembly for a term of eight years, renewable automatically and indefinitely unless disapproved by a two-thirds vote of the total membership of the Legislative Assembly. The court is divided into five chambers, each acting as the appellate court for a specific branch of the law, and sits in plenary session only in cases involving judicial review and impeachment. When the Legislative Assembly considers a law affecting the judicial branch, it must seek the opinion of the Supreme Court. In the event of a lack of agreement by the court, the measure requires a two-thirds vote of the full Assembly in order to become law. The constitution guarantees the full separation of the judicial power, even in the matter of the budget, mandating 6 percent of the annual national budget for the proper functioning of the judiciary. The Supreme Court has demonstrated its independence on numerous occasions, declaring unconstitutional some laws very dear to the other branches, particularly the presidency.

The prestige and respect the Supreme Court of Justice enjoys for its fairness and integrity is not shared by lower courts and in the administration of justice generally. The Supreme Court selects the judges of the lower courts, but the farther down one goes in the system, the more one encounters charges of unfairness and discrimination. According to Mavis, Richard and Karen Biesanz (1979), the poor feel that the rich receive preferential treatment and that judges can be bought. Mitchell Seligson (1980) questions the fairness of the courts in land cases affecting squatters, arguing that the judges represent the "propertied classes." There are no jury trials under the Costa Rican legal system, so judges have great power in the administration of justice and, at the same time, great responsibility. Clearly, in many incidents involving criminal justice (excluding violent crime), the circumstance is not so much a matter of bribing a judge as it is the economic and social status of the party charged, which means there is frequently a resolution *a la tica*. Even in the celebrated case in 1973 concerning the unsuccessful effort to extradite Robert Vesco to the United States, there was no suggestion that the judge in the case had been suborned, but a *tico* friend I talked to winked at me and remarked, "It's a small country, and everyone knows everyone." As previously stated, with reference to the observations of Samuel Stone (1975) there is a "delicate balance" between elitism and egalitarianism in many aspects of *tico* society. In cases of white-collar crime, such as tax evasion, and even in more serious matters, such as dealing in contraband or narcotics violations, there is a relationship between who you are and the manner in which you are punished. There is a sharp contrast between the lofty position the Supreme Court enjoys, on the one hand, and the deep suspicion of the conduct of lower courts, on the other. Maybe *ticos* do not like to admit that they have a crime problem, which may account for the scandalous condition and neglect of Costa Rican prisons until very recent times. The rather low esteem for the judicial system at the grass-roots level is similar to the attitude toward local government in general.

The constitution of 1949 established a unitary republic, with, at latest count, seven provinces, 75 cantons, and 383 districts. The provinces (San José, Cartago, Alajuela, Heredia, Limón, Puntarenas, and Guanacaste) are merely administrative units, and the governor of each is appointed by the president. They have always been subordinate to the central government and, in fact, were ignored completely by OFIPLAN in 1978, when, for purposes of planning and development, it divided the nation into five broad geographical regions: the Central Valley, Atlantic Coast, South Pacific, North Pacific, and northern Plains. The only locally elected bodies of government are the councils of the municipalities, at the canton level. But these, too, have been weak historically, and the constitution of 1949 did little to enhance their status.

The municipalities lack power and prestige because they are dominated by the central government, they do not have adequate, independent sources of revenue, and their functions are ill-defined and overlapping. Until 1970, the presiding officer of the municipal councils — the *jefe político* — was appointed by the president of the republic. The appointed governor acted as the presiding officer over the central canton in each province. In this manner, the central government interfered directly in the activities of the municipalities and exercised a great deal of control over them. The independence of the municipalities is further undermined by the lack of funds. Only about 20 percent of their revenue comes from local sources, such as taxes, fees, and assessments. The remainder is provided by the national government — specifically, the Legislative Assembly, which, in effect, determines what gets done and what does not. However, the problems of the municipalities are compounded by the fact that there is little understanding of what they actually do. The important functions of planning and development and the rendering of essential services, such as education, health and sanitation, housing, roads, water and sewage, and electricity, are all performed either by the ministries of the central government or the autonomous institutions. Most of these have their own local boards or agencies acting completely outside the jurisdiction of the municipalities. The Costa Rican political system is highly centralized, even if the executive branch itself is decentralized.

Christopher Baker, Ronald Fernández Pinto, and Samuel Stone undertook a study of municipal government in Costa Rica in 1972 and discovered that the municipal councils spent 50 to 93 percent of their time in administrative and regulatory matters. They found that local residents did not even use the councils as intermediaries or go-betweens for their problems and petitions, but went directly to the national-government agency involved, such as INVU, on housing; ICE, on electricity; or CCSS, on health care and social services. They suggested that this explained the widespread tax delinquency at the local level (which only added to the decline of the municipalities), and observed that if the strength of democracy is supposed to be based upon strong institutions at the grass-roots level, they were perplexed, because the municipalities, particularly in rural areas, were weak and lacked prestige; they dealt almost exclusively with noncontroversial matters and were not involved in problem resolution. When they attempted to appear to be doing something, such as adding to the body of regulations, they only antagonized local residents and lost what little influence they had.

In an effort to overcome the weakness of local government and to give it a larger role in development, the Costa Rican government reformed the Municipal Code in 1970. The reform provided for an elected municipal executive to preside over the council, although it did not eliminate the *jefe político*, and it established a professional civil service. In the code, the municipal councils were given new responsibilities, for "the promotion of culture, general education, physical and mental health, and public safety and order." In order to aid the municipalities in their tasks, the code created the Institute for Municipal Development and Consultation (IFAM), a new autonomous institution dedicated to planning and interinstitutional coordination. It was designed to provide experts in various fields to municipalities, for consultation, and to provide leverage at the national level. In the ten years that it has been in effect, the Municipal Code of 1970 has not upgraded local government appreciably, because the autonomous institutions continue to have the resources and the influence, while the functions of the municipalities remain ambiguous. In fact, the activities of IFAM generally have duplicated those of DINADECO, and both have frequently found it difficult to obtain the cooperation of the municipalities.

Stone (1975) suggests that this lack of cooperation arises from the composition of the municipal councils themselves. In analyzing their makeup, he discovered that a large percentage of them, particularly in the rural cantons, are dominated by a few rural-elite families, who look upon a seat on the council as a springboard to a seat in the Legislative Assembly. Just as he found a national political class, he perceives a local political class, but, whereas the national elites are motivated by civic responsibility, the local elites are seeking to satisfy their own political ambitions. In the 1966-70 Legislative Assembly, 23 of the 57 deputies had served on municipal councils. This has meant that, as municipal-council members (*regidores*), they have tended to sacrifice local needs for national political considerations, further diminishing the effectiveness and standing of the municipalities.

Although local government appears weak, it is clear that the constitution of 1949 contains an effective system of checks and balances and provides for the separation of powers. Some scholars, such as Charles Denton (1971), think the system of checks and balances is too effective, to the point of "immobilizing" the Costa Rican government and making it difficult to make decisions. The Biesanzes (1979) concur and add that Costa Rica's democratic safeguards contribute more to stability than to efficiency. Stone points out that the mechanism of the welfare state has become so powerful that neither the PLN nor its opposition is able to control it. However, it is also true that the concept of state responsibility for economic development and social well-being is now widely accepted. The machinery of government and the institutionalized reform tell only half the story. Despite the restraints, politicians and political parties have plenty of opportunity to maneuver. Moreover, in a country like Costa Rica, with its family ties, informal arrangements, and cult of personality, institutions provide legitimacy but not all the answers. The other half of the story rests in the political dynamics of Costa Rica, where the struggle for power really takes place.

4

POLITICAL DYNAMICS:
THE SHIRT-SLEEVE DEMOCRACY

Ticos have faith in the strength of their political process. There is no official party in control, and the political outs, free to campaign for office, have confidence that they can win. This situation may be attributed to the effectiveness of the Supreme Electoral Tribunal (TSE) and to the respect it enjoys. As already noted, the TSE functions independently of any other branch of government and is completely in control of the conduct of political campaigns and the management of elections. In its added role as the nation's civil register, it virtually has eliminated fraud in Costa Rican elections. It determines the start of the political-campaign season — officially, six months before election day, although political campaigning never really ends — and monitors campaigns carefully in order to enforce the electoral laws and avoid unfair practices. The electoral laws are strict and include the observance of absolute impartiality on the part of the government and its officers, the requirement that government officials resign in order to be candidates for elective office, and the rule that rival parties may not schedule rallies in the same location or town on the same day. The TSE receives and investigates complaints and acts against violators. It is in charge of the disbursement of campaign funds, in accordance with Costa

57

Rica's public-campaign funding law, which generally has reduced the power and influence of moneyed interests and has overcome political graft and corruption. When the campaign is over, the TSE counts the ballots and as noted before, is the sole power with the authority to announce and certify the results.

The Supreme Electoral Tribunal does more, of course, than see to it that electoral fraud does not occur. It makes certain that those with the franchise are free to exercise it. Proper credentials, convenient and accessible polling places, and the secret ballot help to ensure this, but the TSE protects the voter against any type of coercion or influence by the ruling government. It is also protective toward civil servants, and, in this regard, the law prohibits any sort of political-campaign activity in public offices, including the wearing of campaign buttons by public employees. Voting is compulsory in Costa Rica and, despite the fact that the penalties are light and rarely enforced, approximately 80 percent of the electorate goes to the polls. Although every effort is made to protect the secrecy of the ballot, *ticos* feel free to display their political sympathies, confident that they live in a democracy. They take an active part in the campaigns and say publicly how they intend to vote.

Costa Rican elections are held every four years — the first Sunday in February — at which time the *ticos* choose a president, two vice presidents, congressional deputies, and municipal representatives. Costa Rican campaign methods are relatively simple. Preelectoral polling by political parties, to determine voter attitudes, is not yet practiced. But *ticos* make up in enthusiasm what they lack in technique. Political parties spend a great deal of money in media advertising — in newspapers, radio, and television — although the media, especially newspapers, are blatantly partisan and give their choices ample free coverage. Political parties are identified by specific colors, which their partisans display in various ways. Flags and banners with party colors are particularly popular and flutter from poles, trees, and TV antennas. Neighbors compete with one another for the tallest flagstaff, creating a literal forest above the rooftops of the cities and towns. Badges, buttons, bumper stickers, sound trucks, and balloons add to the spirit of the occasion. On election day, appropriately decorated automobiles, vans, and trucks take shut-ins and rural folk to the polls, where young people who

wear T-shirts displaying the colors and name of their favorite dis-
tribute campaign literature. Boy Scouts and Girl Scouts are also
on hand to assist voters, although their role is nonpartisan. The
presidential candidates of the major parties crisscross the tiny
country numerous times, traveling in four-wheel-drive vehicles and
in helicopters to reach even the most remote villages. Political
parties traditionally publish long lists of names of their adherents,
along with huge photographs of the crowds at their rallies. Political
rallies are social events, too, and everyone enjoys the civic festival.
Following the speeches, especially in the smaller towns, the
candidate and the party faithful share an evening of dining, drinking,
and dancing.

One explanation for this phenomenon is the highly personalistic
and informal character of *tico* politics. Despite the emergence of
political parties and ideological positions, personalities are still
significant, and *ticos* frequently switch party affiliations in order
to follow an individual. Candidates are addressed as, say, "Don
Pepe" and "Don Rodrigo" and appear in public in open collars
and shirt-sleeves. Costa Rica is indeed the shirt-sleeve democracy.
Candidates mingle freely among the people, accompanied by only
one or two companions serving as bodyguards. In fact, it is more
often the candidate who may assault a heckler than the other way
around. Personalism produces adoring crowds, but it also causes
mudslinging, and campaigns are notoriously dirty, the efforts of
the TSE notwithstanding. For example, in the election of 1966,
the opposition accused Daniel Oduber, the National Liberation
candidate, of being a thief, a Communist, and a friend of Fidel
Castro's, which may have caused his defeat, because the election
was very close. He subsequently cleared his name in a libel suit
against *La Nación*, the principal opposition newspaper. However,
in an individualistic society like Costa Rica's, name-calling is a
tactic too effective to abandon. Critics of Costa Rican democracy
charge that this kind of activity demonstrates the meaninglessness
of Costa Rican politics. They concede that the popular classes may
have some fun and get to cast a ballot, but they affirm that they
have no real power and are able merely to choose from among
candidates preselected by the affluent groups. This charge, although
serious, is as superficial as the campaign hoopla it criticizes.
Personalism remains a potent force in Costa Rican politics, but it

may no longer be dominant, and the functioning of the National Liberation Party (PLN) has contributed to this change.

The PLN, founded in 1951, is the oldest continuous party in Costa Rica today. Its origins may be traced to the so-called generation of 1940, which sought to create a more equitable and efficient society, while maintaining and strengthening Costa Rica's democratic institutions. However, the PLN's strength and weakness lie in the military victory of 1948 and the leadership of José Figueres. Lacking ideological unity, because of the varying backgrounds of its founders, the party has taken shape through the exercise of political power and has demonstrated a high degree of pragmatism. It has been described variously as social democratic and as authoritarian transformist. Of these descriptions, the authoritarian one is out of place. Only once between 1953 and the present did the PLN succeed itself in the presidency and on no occasion did it attempt to thwart the popular will. In addition to occupying the presidency four times since the period of the founding junta, the party controlled the Legislative Assembly, without interruption, between 1953 and 1978. The PLN's individual leaders have powerful influence, but even Figueres has not always had his way. His principal weapon has been the threat to bolt from the party and present an independent candidacy, but he has not carried it out. In the meantime, he has aged and has made serious mistakes, which increase the PLN's chances to survive without him. One heard talk of a "troika" during the 1960's, comprised of Figueres, Orlich, and Oduber. This implied the existence of an informal power structure within the PLN, but also signaled a dispersal of power and a circumstance distinct from the one-man parties of former times. Within the context of its internal power struggle and the existence of a dynamic situation, the PLN increasingly has assumed an identity of its own.

The PLN has a permanent secretariat, with a party secretary and offices, and a functioning committee structure. It does not suddenly appear six months before the elections and disappear after them, as is the case with most other parties. It maintains publishing and educational activities and has special-interest sections for women, labor, and youth. The influence of these groups upon party policy is variable, but women are active, and an impressive number of them hold high party positions, are nominated for elective office, and have occupied important government posts, including those of ministerial rank. The party nominates major candidates at a convention, and the presidential nomination is frequently hotly contested, as in 1970. Costa Rica's campaign-funding laws have had a profound effect upon the PLN's selection of candidates for deputy, especially in rural areas. No longer dependent on the rural elites for funds, the party may seek the most effective candidates. This may or may not be more democratic, because national party considerations may overrule local needs, but at least factors other than money come into play. Stone (1975) suggests that the party has replaced the local political class, tending to further weaken local government. On the other hand, people join the party as a means of resolving local problems and for furthering political ambitions, and not simply to follow a particular leader. In the Legislative Assembly, PLN deputies have maintained a degree of unity, but party discipline has been inconsistent, largely because of the constitutional provision preventing reelection. Nonetheless, those ambitious for political careers have a stake in the party's success.

The PLN has become closely identified with the existing system of government. The welfare state, or the concept of governmental responsibility for economic and social well-being, is associated with the policy and the terms of office of PLN presidents. The PLN has been responsible for extending the role of government and for enlarging the public sector since 1950, so its situation bears some analogy to that of the Institutional Revolutionary Party (PRI) in Mexico, and the opposition, in attacking the PLN, must be careful not to appear to be attacking the very essence of government. Although public employees are hired and protected under a civil-service system, they are aware of the PLN's role in creating their jobs, and a vast majority of them are Liberacionistas. In fact, the PLN has been accused of expanding the bureaucracy as a means of maintaining political stability and heading off radical activity on the part of university youth and intellectuals. However, this has been a two-edged sword. The bureaucracy, in turn, exercises a powerful influence upon the PLN and has given it a middle-class orientation, although it is one that is based heavily in the public sector. The labor and peasant sectors are vastly weaker.

The degree to which National Liberation is internally democratic is a matter of controversy, but there is no question that there is an internal dynamic. As long as PLN doctrine enjoys a broad national consensus, the party will be able to keep ambitious politicians in line, through the promise of elective office and ministerial careers, and it will maintain the support of the bureaucracy because it is its best hope. Again, the influence of personalism may be fading and may continue to do so because the constitution prohibits re-election. As the number of living ex-presidents increases, power will be dispersed, as each attempts to influence party councils, unless one finds a suitable alternative, such as a protégé or surrogate. There is little profit, however, in being a spoiler, because the party knows, through experience, the rewards of unity. Ever since 1953 – win or lose – the party has managed to capture at least 40 percent of the vote, the minimum required by the constitution for electing a president. The figure of the principal founder, Figueres, remains a factor, but his reputation was seriously damaged by his association with Vesco during his last presidency (1970-74). Figueres and Oduber, the PLN's other living ex-president, are bitter enemies, and, divided as such, have been unable to prevent the rise of Luis Alberto Monge. Monge, who overcame defeat in 1978 and won the presidency in 1982, is beholden to neither of them and is a product of the party, having risen through the ranks and having served as party secretary for a number of years. Critics charge that the PLN has lost its way; but Monge, with trade-union experience and no strong ties to the private sector, represents a regeneration of social-democratic philosophy. Unlike Figueres and Oduber, Monge is not a landowner interested in agribusiness. If the PLN can survive the passing of its old guard, the future of party politics in Costa Rica in general may be different from what it has been in the past.

During the time that National Liberation has dominated Costa Rican politics, other political parties have come and gone. Otilio Ulate's National Union Party (PUN) is the only party that has been able to defeat the PLN single-handedly since 1953. Indeed, it won in 1958, when Mario Echandi defeated Francisco Orlich, but only because it enjoyed the silent support of Calderón's outlawed Republican Party, while the immature PLN experienced a split, which led to the breakaway candidacy of Jorge Rossi. When the PLN patched up its differences, Orlich won handily in 1962. This time, Ulate, himself running as a candidate, placed a distant third behind Calderón, who returned from exile to reenter electoral politics.

Because of the highly personalistic nature of the PUN, it disappeared completely when Ulate died in 1973. Calderón, despite his military defeat in 1948 and his subsequent efforts in December 1948 and January 1955 to overthrow the Figueres governments, with the assistance of Nicaraguan dictator Anastasio Somoza, remained a popular leader in Costa Rica until the time of his death in 1970. His political comeback in 1962, when he captured 35 percent of the vote, demonstrated his hold over the banana workers and the urban poor, particularly. He revived the old Republican Party label, but it was *calderonismo*, identified with Calderón's social legislation of the 1940's that accounted for his continued popularity and made him the PLN's most formidable foe. Even following his death, the renamed Calderonista Republican Party remained strong, and Calderón's son, Rafael Angel Claderón Fournier, known as "Junior" Calderón, eventually assumed the party leadership and emerged as a presidential candidate. Beginning in 1966, however, the Calderonistas did not present an independent candidacy, but participated in various anti-PLN coalitions, which placed them with strange bedfellows. Except for the hate engendered by the 1948 civil war, the Calderonistas have more in common with the PLN than with the groups with which they have collaborated.

Because of the dominance of the PLN and the constitutional provision that a presidential candidate needs 40 percent of the vote in order to be elected, opposition parties have resorted to coalition politics as a means of making an effective challenge. Although Costa Rica has not as yet evolved a two-party system, the fact that the nation is closely divided between Liberación and anti-Liberación has, at times, produced a similar effect. The defeats the PLN suffered in 1966 and 1978 were administered by coalitions of opposition parties. The coalitions were not identical, although certain parties participated in both. In 1966, Calderón and Ulate joined forces to form the National Unification Party (not to be confused with Ulate's National Union Party) and successfully supported the candidacy of José Joaquín Trejos Fernández. The election was extremely close, with Unification capturing 50.5 percent of the vote and Liberación, 49.5 percent — demonstrating to both contestants the importance of unity.

Despite this lesson, Unification did not stay intact, and lost the next three elections. The disparate elements making up the coalition, combined with the ambition, ego, and vanity of its leaders, resulted in its steady decline, to the extent that, for the first time since the PLN's founding, it succeeded itself in the presidency in 1974. In 1978, Unification was not even part of the new and victorious coalition. Unification suffered its first serious defection in 1970, when Ulate withdrew to present his last hurrah. In 1974, despite the fact that the PLN received its lowest percentage of the total vote since its founding (42.5 percent), Unification could not prevail (it received only 30 percent of the vote), because of the independent candidacies of ambitious politicians, especially those of Jorge González Martén and Rodrigo Carazo Odio. Four years later, it refused to join the new Unity Party coalition, probably because of the campaign-funding law (it had received over 10 percent of the vote in the previous election and was entitled to advance funding), and, although no longer a viable party, had all the money it needed. It wound up with less than 2 percent of the vote and its demise was complete, but already a new coalition had taken its place.

The Unity Party coalition won the election of 1978, with Rodrigo Carazo as its candidate. Carazo had been a rising young leader in the PLN, but left the party in 1970, following his unsuccessful challenge of Figueres for the party's nomination. For the 1974 election, he founded his own party, called Democratic Renovation and made up of a few disaffected Liberacionistas – particularly the younger persons tired of old-guard domination and angered by the perceived corruption of the Figueres administration – but aided also by oligarchical groups anxious to promote schisms within the PLN. He ran a distant fourth in the 1974 election (receiving just under 10 percent of the vote), but continued evidence of corruption in the PLN government of Oduber increased his following and enabled him to persuade the Calderonistas to abandon the dying National Unification Party. Carazo was in a position to capitalize on the corruption issue without appearing to be hostile to Liberación doctrine, and he could bring together a more compatible coalition of youthful Liberacionistas and Calderonistas, which had not been possible under the old guard, because the latter kept alive the bitterness of 1948. Moreover, the Calderonista leader – Junior Calderón – was too young himself for the presidency, but, by becoming part of what appeared to be a promising coalition, was staking his claim on the future.

Carazo also managed to attract the small Christian Democratic Party, as well as a nonparty supported by the oligarchy and called the Popular Union Party. The Christian Democrats had appeared on the ballot for the first time in 1974 and represented a new and untested element in *tico* politics. Similarly, the Popular Union Party appeared in 1974 — marking a more visible participation in politics on the part of the coffee barons than had been the case for a number of years — although it presented no candidates of its own, even for deputy. Popular Union took part in the Unification coalition in 1974, but, displaying keen political sense, switched to Unity in 1978. Despite the fact that Monge received a higher percentage of the vote than Oduber had in victory four years earlier, Carazo and Unity won in 1978 with just over 50 percent of the total votes cast.

Unity's victory in 1978 revived speculation that Costa Rica was moving toward a two-party system. Politicians recognized the fact that the only way to combat the PLN effectively was through a unified opposition. Nonetheless, despite the obvious, the parties making up the Unity coalition continue to maintain their specific identity. The members of the Council of Government (the cabinet) bear their individual party labels, and the parties are listed separately in the San José telephone directory. Moreover, Unity does not appear to have a well-defined organization. There is no permanent party headquarters, nor are there activities at the grass-roots level. During the first half of Carazo's administration, Unity's momentum appeared to be holding up, but after 1980, fissures appeared, partly owing to Carazo's declining popularity and partly because of the nation's growing economic problems.

Upon taking office, Carazo compared himself to President Jimmy Carter, whom he admired, even noting the similarity of their toothy smiles. However, as Carter's position deteriorated in the United States, the comparison became an unfortunate one, because Carazo's own mistakes were magnified and characterized as stemming from a shared ineptitude. In addition, the issue of corruption persisted, particularly Carazo's alleged profiteering in contraband-arms sales to the Sandinistas in Nicaragua, and Carazo found himself the target of his own rhetoric. The growing problems of Costa Rica's economy (to be discussed later) and Carazo's inability to deal with them effectively further weakened Unity. Ironically, the continued division within the PLN itself also undermined the Unity coalition, as ambitious leaders were tempted to strike out on their own, perceiving less need to remain with the pack when the lion is wounded.

The future of a two-party system depends upon the strength of Liberación, which, as a further irony, is better served by a multi-party system; that is, in the elections of 1974 and 1978 it obtained less than 45 percent of the vote. These results are a more accurate measure of PLN strength than the large total amassed by Monge in 1982, which, as will be seen, stemmed from extraordinary circumstances. Monge may have actually been helped in 1982 by the defection of Gonzalo Facio, a longtime Liberacionista leader and Oduber's foreign minister, who had announced an independent candidacy. Given the recent history of political parties in Costa Rica, and the ever-present force of personalism, Liberación may be in trouble, but the odds against the survival of Unity in its present form are even longer. In any case, a persistent criticism of the main political parties is that they are too alike, that they are dominated by urban, upper-middle-class males and provide little opportunity for participation by the popular classes. Left-wing parties have tried to exploit this criticism, but without a great deal of success.

Until now, the Communist and socialist movements in Costa Rica have been small and insignificant. The Communist Party, founded officially in 1931, has never attracted more than a handful of votes in national elections. During the "eight years" (the period of Calderón's rule), when it enjoyed its greatest success, it changed its name and renounced its own program and defined ideology. After the 1948 civil war, the Communist Party, or Popular Vanguard, was outlawed until 1975, but it continued to take part in politics under labels of various front organizations, and the existing governments never seriously bothered it. The fact that the Communist Party has appeared to be more a curiosity than a threat may account for the casual attitude toward it. Another reason is the party's leader, Manuel Mora Valverde, the only leader the party has ever had. Mora gives the Communists a personalistic touch, to the extent that he is a fixture in Costa Rican politics, and many *ticos* feel comfortable with him. Many non-Communists respect him as an intellectual and a tenacious idealist and vote for him. Mora, in turn, does not frighten most *ticos*. He has stated that a true revolution must take root in a nation's own soil and has declared that he would never violate "the good national traditions" (Barahona, 1971).

The rather benign nature of *tico* communism led to defections within its ranks, particularly toward the end of the sixties and the beginning of the seventies, when youthful Marxists took a more militant stand. They were dissatisfied as much with Mora's leadership *a la tica* as they were with the rule of the major parties. The young Marxists in Costa Rica were similar to their counterparts around the globe in the Vietnam era. They were independent and schismatic. A number of Marxist parties appeared on the ballot in 1970 and 1974, and the Marxists seemed to be as divided as any group on the political spectrum. However, in 1978, the Popular Vanguard and the Costa Rican Socialist Party, principally, imitated their bourgeois rivals and formed a coalition, the United Peoples Party. Although the United Peoples Party ran a very distant third in the presidential election, gaining less than 3 percent of the vote, it managed to elect three deputies to the Legislative Assembly. Given the fact that Unity had 27 deputies, and PLN 25, (there were also two independent seats in the 57-seat chamber), the three Marxist deputies exercised inordinate influence, which encouraged the United Peoples coalition and may help to convert it into a third party. In any case, the leadership of Mora is passing, and *tico* Marxism is more hardline now than it has been for 20 years. This presents a new challenge for *tico* democracy, given recent events in Nicaragua and the rest of Central America.

At the same time, *tico* democracy has faced the challenge of the political right. Costa Rica's right has operated generally through individual parties or participated in the various anti-PLN coalitions, but its most extreme element has organized as a pressure group and has resorted to intimidation, propaganda, and, on at least one occasion, subversion. The Free Costa Rica Movement (MCRL), or Costa Rica Libre, founded in the late sixties by Costa Rica's more adventurous types, is a militantly anti-Communist organization that seems more determined to suppress *tico* democracy than to preserve it. Though seemingly out of place in Costa Rican society, violence-prone individuals and persons inclined to use force in political affairs do exist. Costa Rica Libre became especially threatening in late 1970 and early 1971, during the controversy over

Figueres's establishment of diplomatic relations with the Soviet Union. The MCRL held weekend encampments, where its members received military training in preparation for a coup against the Figueres government in February 1971. Although the coup was thwarted, reports about it revealed ties between MCRL and Mano Blanco, an anti-Communist extremist organization in Guatemala. These events took place ten years ago, but indicate that the Costa Rican right, just like the left, has international links and that, in any Central American crisis, *tico* democracy must be vigilant against both.

Costa Rica Libre, as a pressure group, albeit a more militant one, brings into focus another important element of Costa Rican politics. Pressure groups are, according to Oscar Arias Sánchez (1971) a "way of life" in Costa Rica. The nation's generally weak political-party system, combined with its decentralized administrative structure, provides unusual opportunities for influence by special interests. Both bureaucrats and deputies have decision-making power, but frequently exercise it loosely, given the weakness of the presidency and the lack of party discipline. Well-organized pressure groups are able to prey upon this circumstance. They include chambers of commerce, organizations of producers of various agricultural products, professional associations, employee organizations and unions, as well as cooperatives, autonomous institutions, and state agencies and enterprises. Pressure groups represent both the public and private sectors, so that the individual's voice in Costa Rican politics is muted. Arias, who has analyzed these groups, believes that they constitute a threat to *tico* democracy. He affirms that businessmen, for example, are overrepresented through pressure-group activity, while the poor, the aged, and the ill are not represented at all.

The nation's most powerful pressure group is the National Association for Economic Development (ANFE), which is underwritten by the business community and expresses conservative economic and political viewpoints. It sponsors a daily column of economic and political commentary in *La Nación*, Costa Rica's largest newspaper, and spends additional money in the print media and for supporting political candidates of its choice. Because of their individualistic nature, *tico* businessmen tend to remain small, limiting their investments and shunning the corporate form of business organization and large-scale enterprises. They are neither risk takers nor moguls. As a result, in order to enhance their influence, they form associations or chambers and state their position collectively. While ANFE is the strongest of these, there are also the Costa Rican Chamber of Commerce, the National Chamber of Coffee Producers, and the Guanacaste Cattlemen's Association, to name just a few. *Ticos*, by nature, are not joiners, but the political success realized by pressure groups is overcoming this attitude. Even professional persons, such as medical doctors, with their College of Physicians and Surgeons, have recognized that they are stronger acting as a group than alone.

The pressure groups vary in size, resources, and composition. Their methods and purposes are also distinct. The College of Lawyers may be smaller than the Federation of Costa Rican Students (FECR), but it has better contacts. ANFE and MCRL, with a small membership but heavy financing, can match the National Association of Public Employees (ANEP), despite ANEP's membership of approximately 2,500 persons. Persuasion through advertising and propaganda is the most common and visible form of pressure-group activity. In 1967, *tico* business and financial sectors formed the Committee for Private Banking and conducted an all-out campaign to achieve the repeal of the nationalized banking law. Although eventually defeated, this effort was one of the most intense and best-financed pressure-group activities in Costa Rican history, including a media blitz, door-to-door and letter-writing campaigns, and public lectures and rallies. This was probably the most serious attack upon the PLN structure of government since the 1948 civil war. Pressure groups undoubtedly employ covert and subtle tactics, which may be easily imagined in a society where *sangre* and the informal and polite way of conflict resolution are valued, but there have been no major scandals involving pressure groups in practices of intimidation and corruption, even though the latter is widely speculated upon and assumed to exist. Clearly, the opportunity for pressure groups to influence or threaten elected officials is diminished by the public financing of political campaigns and by the prescription against the reelection of deputies. Aside from persuasion, the tactics of pressure groups involve mostly direct action.

The principal form of direct action is the strike. It is particularly effective when it involves the public sector and, consequently, the inconveniencing of the public at large. Though organized labor is not strong in Costa Rica, public employees, whether organized by profession or vocation, or within a particular autonomous institution, have exercised important influence over political affairs. Because of the large public sector, strikes by public employees that are solely for better wages or working conditions affect the economy and shape policy in countless and unpredictable ways. As a pressure group, public employees can make demands upon the national budget that few other elements in society can equal, and simply by protecting their jobs, they determine the structure of government itself. They are the new status quo, fighting for their interests and generally resisting change. PLN leaders, such as Figueres, deplore this situation as an undesirable outcome of their programs and policies and have tried to enforce and strengthen laws prohibiting strikes by public employees, but with little success. The PLN feels that a strike or a threat of one by public employees amounts to a sabotaging of the political system, but such strikes have become as much a part of the political dynamic as has party activity.

Outside of the political parties and organized pressure groups, the degree to which specific elements of society or institutions influence Costa Rican politics is generally insignificant. Institutions such as the church and the military lack power, and organizations composed solely of workers, peasants, women, or youth either do not exist or are ineffective. Costa Rica is a pluralistic society, so loyalties and interests are very diverse, but the *tico* way and individualism likewise explain the weakness of such organizations, as do the functioning of the welfare state and paternalism.

Organized labor, for example, is weak because it is divided and lacks appeal. There are three national labor confederations – one for each of the party lines, that is: the Confederation of Democratic Workers (Social Democratic, or PLN); the General Confederation of Workers (Communist); and the Confederation of Christian Workers and Peasants (Christian Democratic). Yet, the total membership of these is less than 20,000. *Ticos* reject the class struggle and generally prefer to resolve labor disputes amicably. The PLN, although the sponsor of the Democratic Workers Confederation, embraces the multiclass concept and promotes the idea of increased productivity through class harmony. The powerful teachers' union, ANDE, and the National Association of Public Employees shun the confederations on the basis that they are too radical. The teachers may strike against the impersonal state, but, in their opinion, it is merely a tactic that has nothing to do with the class struggle, and their attitude is strictly middle class. Organized labor is also handicapped by the existence of the welfare state. The Labor Code and social guarantees leave little for the labor organizer to offer. Wages, hours, working conditions, benefits, and rights are indeed so thoroughly governed by legislation that workers have little incentive to organize. Disputes are resolved in the courts, in accordance with the law (the Labor Code). In many small businesses, such as *beneficios*, paternalism is virtually a cultural trait, and workers frequently value the personal relationship with the *patrón* above all else. It is not uncommon for workers in rural areas to work for less for an employer whom they like and respect than for one who may offer more money but lacks a common touch. Organized labor in Costa Rica does better in impersonal situations; therefore, as the country becomes more industrialized, the labor picture may change.

One may infer this from the initial success of labor unions in the banana regions. The nature and relationship of labor and management there provided a more classic setting for the rise of organized labor. However, the development of unions among the banana workers is also associated with the rise of the Communist Party and a collaboration with Rafael Angel Calderón Guardia in the 1940's. This circumstance has undermined the influence of the banana workers' unions, and the PLN has tried to establish the superiority of the economic mechanisms of the state over the unions. The Labor Code specifically defines labor-management relations, including the right to strike. Moreover, during his first administration, Figueres renegotiated the contracts of the fruit companies and fixed new conditions for their operations in Costa Rica. As part of the package, he made a wage settlement, serving, in effect, as the barganing agent for the workers. Although Figueres believed that he acted in the best interests of the workers, he made it clear that the workers' interests were only one of the considerations in the settlement. This situation has been aggravated by the expansion of the public sector in the banana regions, through the activities of the Atlantic Coast Port Authority (JAPDEVA), the nationalization of the Northern Railway, and the creation of a state banana enterprise. Despite the state's assumption of responsibility for the well-being of the banana workers, as a result of the PLN's action, the banana workers remain hostile toward the PLN. In fact, Liberación does poorly in elections in the banana provinces of Limón and Puntarenas, and voter absention is high in these two places. Essentially, although looking upon itself as pro-labor, the philosophy and programs of the PLN are incompatible with trade unionism, as is, consequently, the structure of *tico* government.

If workers, as a group, lack influence in politics, the situation of peasants is more dismal. The yeoman farmer, at one time the back-bone of *tico* democracy, has been disappearing in Costa Rica. The rise of coffee and similar export products helped to concentrate land into the hands of fewer persons and led to a situation today in which approximately 78 percent of the peasants are landless. The parties campaign hard for the peasants' votes and promise to improve their position, but peasants themselves lack effective means for influencing political programs and decisions. The PLN, for example, is generally successful in winning the votes of peasants, but has never presented an agrarian program that bears the imprint of peasant thinking. The availability of public funds for political campaigns has enabled parties, especially the PLN, to select local candidates on a basis other than of wealth. In this way, the party has replaced the local elites as benefactor, and peasants have gained some political power within the confines of party organization. No important peasant organizations have developed, other than a few small groups concerned with land acquisition.

The peasants' main objective in recent years has been to acquire land, but the methods and techniques have been developed externally. Government programs, undertaken by the Institute of Lands and Colonization (ITCO), have avoided land redistribution, trying, instead, colonization schemes; programs to enable squatters and renters to secure land titles; and the organization of agricul-tural settlements (in developed areas). During the seventies, the Communist Party helped to establish peasant leagues, whose main purpose was to plan and organize land occupations. Some violence accompanied these actions, but the failure to plan beyond the actual seizures led to internal dissension and to the decline of the leagues. The presence of the Communists also undermined the leagues, although most peasant leaders resisted their influence. More recently, the Christian Democrats, through the formation of the Confederation of Christian Workers and Peasants, have tried to organize the peasants, but with only limited success. It is curious that Costa Rican peasants have not been more active politically, given the steady decline of their position, but actually, the development of what Mitchell Seligson (1980) calls agrarian capitalism has been gradual, and, in the meantime, Costa Rican political democracy has been functioning; that is, civil and human rights have been observed and there have been no tensions based upon race or status. Moreover, peasants have had certain options, such as working for wages or migrating to the cities. The peasant, like most Costa Ricans, has not developed a strong class consciousness, so one may observe his leaders working within the existing political parties – the PLN, for example – rather than forming a specific group for direct action.

The political influence of the Catholic church also appears to be more indirect than direct. Nine out of ten *ticos* are Catholic, but for many, the tie is emotional and does not translate into specific action in the political arena. The influence of the church upon public morality is manifest, being observed in such matters as religious instruction in the schools and the existence of strict divorce laws. However, in the late sixties, the church offered only token opposition to state programs for family planning, and, indeed, José Figueres's divorce was never a political issue. The church is poor, the number of clergy is small, and the state has taken over most social and welfare activities, including dealing with family and domestic problems, alcoholism, and prostitution. The anticlericalism of the liberal reformers of the nineteenth century and of the Olympians of the twentieth essentially fixed the political status of the church. Only occasionally has it broken its restraint through the activism of individual clerics, such as Bishop Thiel, Jorge Volio, and Archbishop Sanabria. Sanabria, who collaborated with Calderón and Mora in the 1940s, involved the church in economic and social reform. In the early forties, he was responsible for the formation of the Rerum Novarum labor confederation and assigned a young priest, Benjamín Núñez, to direct it. Subsequently, Núñez joined Figueres's guerrilla army and served on the founding junta. He was also a founder of the PLN and remains to this day one of its principal leaders. Generally, however, the church is conservative; that is, few of the higher clergy today share Sanabria's philosophy, and younger, activist priests have had to be content with involvement in community programs and rural development, rather than in political activity. The appearance of the Christian Democratic Party in 1974 and the founding of the Confederation of Christian Workers and Peasants earlier may have signaled a more active political role for the church or for organized Catholic laypersons. Women have provided leadership in the public policies of the church; and the Civic League of Costa Rican Women organized an impressive demonstration against the establishment of the Soviet embassy in San José in 1970.

One of the reasons that Ricardo Jiménez opposed women's suffrage was his fear that it would strengthen the Catholic church. As it turned out, the principal beneficiary of the vote for women has been the PLN, not the church. Women's organizations are not influential in Costa Rica, but politically active women have found a place in the PLN. National Liberation fought for women's suffrage and has been responsible for gaining rights for women in many areas, including legal guarantees for married women, especially in economic matters, and equal pay for equal work. The PLN has proved to be very sensitive to women's issues, and women themselves have had a direct role in the formulation of policy. Outside of party activity, however, Costa Rican women are not politically strong. Even the PLN has to plead with its male partisans, especially in rural areas, to permit their wives to go to the polls to vote. Many *ticos* lock their wives in the house on election day, but *machismo* is not the only problem. The Biesanzes (1979) describe the persistence of *marianismo*, in which women find virtue in the ability to bear stoically their disappointments in marriage; the worse the male, the stronger the female. Since the church tends to promote these sex roles, Don Ricardo's fears were groundless, because Costa Rican women, while still short of equality, have been a factor in reform, principally through participation in the PLN. Although women in Costa Rica are more active politically than women in other countries of Latin America, *tico* youth have been less active in comparison.

Student activism, particularly among university students, is virtually a stereotype in Latin America, but the campus of the University of Costa Rica is generally staid and quiet. To be sure, there are more activists and radicals among Costa Rican youth than among their elders. In April 1970, the Legislative Assembly's decision to grant a concession to the Aluminum Company of

America (Alcoa) for the exploitation of bauxite resulted in a violent demonstration by university and secondary-school youth. During his second administration (1970-74), Figueres stopped coming to UCR because of the taunts and jeers of the students. The Nicaraguan crisis in 1979 and the events in El Salvador more recently have stirred university students, who have shown their sympathies by means of rallies, signs, posters, and graffiti. It is a kind of bourgeois radicalism, however, that ceases after college. The incidents that have occurred are isolated, and Costa Rican youth generally are not well organized.

The Federation of Costa Rican Students (FECR) is the only significant organization of young people, and it has been successful occasionally in pressuring the government to meet its demands. UCR is an autonomous institution, and students have demonstrated in behalf of its budget allocation and administrative integrity. The university, however, is essentially a conservative institution, because its limited enrollment has created a long waiting list, with the result that students matriculate at an older age, and there is a sense of elitism. The hope for a government job is also a stabilizing influence, and, being aware of this, the state (the PLN especially) has continued to expand the bureaucracy. In order to meet growing demands for college admissions, Figueres inaugurated the National University at Heredia in 1972, and appointed Núñez as its first rector. Núñez, more liberal in his views, criticized the alleged elitism of UCR and adopted a policy of open admissions. He also made a number of controversial faculty appointments, especially those involving Chilean refugees, following the fall of Salvador Allende. The National University became the working person's university, but conservatives attacked it as radical, and its practice of not turning away students strained its budget. Nonetheless, even the students of the National University look upon education as a means of personal advancement — specifically, the obtaining of a white-collar position — and only a small number are serious activists.

Politically ambitious youth recognize the advantages of affiliation with the established parties, but generally lack influence in party councils. This is a bit surprising, given the youthfulness of the Costa Rican population and the fact that the voting age is 18. The PLN's youth group, Liberacionista Youth, takes part in educating, organizing, and mobilizing young people, but exercises little power. During the sixties and seventies, there was a noticeable generation gap in the PLN, triggered by the Cuban revolution. Figueres, an outspoken critic of Fidel Castro, admonished Costa Rican youth about "going into the hills" and counseled patience, suggesting that young people engage in constructive works and stay in school (Ameringer, 1979). Figueres's patronizing attitude was resented by many youths, and Liberacionista Youth grew restive under the domination of the old guard. Carazo's challenge of Figueres for the 1970 PLN presidential nomination marked the culmination of this movement. Unfortunately, Carazo was virtually forced to leave the PLN, and many of the PLN's young leaders joined him. In an attempt to win back youth and show sensitivity for its concerns, Figueres created the Ministry of Culture, Youth, and Sports in 1972. Although the ministry is providing leadership in the resolution of economic and social problems peculiar to youth, the role of youth itself is a passive one.

It is evident that political power remains in the hands of those who have exercised it in Costa Rica since colonial times. As Stone (1975) points out, seven of the ten candidates for president in the elections between 1958 and 1970 were descendants of the colonial founder Vásquez de Coronado. This does not imply that there is a narrow, closed elite. It means that the *sangre* and family ties remain important in *tico* politics, even though the so-called class is dispersed along the political spectrum. The ruling class in Costa Rica has been very adaptive and may be found on both sides of the predominant trends in politics: the reformist (PLN), and the conservative (the opposition coalitions). Stone believes that family is very important in gaining access to political power. It accounts for the continuing strength of personalism in politics and for the prevailing phenomenon of personal contacts of pull – *la palanca* – in *tico* affairs. At the same time, the human factor alone does not explain the exercise of political power.

The institutional framework that has evolved since 1949 places restraints upon human performance. Power is widely dispersed within the executive branch, and the autonomous institutions exercise great freedom. Arias (1971) has noted that the system is particularly vulnerable to pressure-group activity, and he thus fears for the future of Costa Rican democracy. The PLN, principally, has dominated affairs for the last 30 years, representing the weak and exploited elements in society and shaping the welfare state. This probably accounts in part for the absence of significant pressure-group activity by these elements. On the other hand, reforms develop abuses of their own, and 30 years of power do corrupt. Critics of the PLN say it has "lost its way," but it may be more accurate to say that it has wrought great change and that some of that change is producing new problems. The PLN, particularly the old guard, finds it difficult to correct what it has believed in for so long.

Political dynamics are by definition a fluid circumstance. Whereas many elements once found satisfaction in the PLN, they are now being challenged for power by the new middle class created by the expanded bureaucracy. The PLN's leadership has also profited by the system, and the quest for personal gain and a suspicion of corruption are debilitating the party. Costa Rican politics are approaching something of a crisis. The oldest continuous party needs to revitalize itself and is faced with a need to restudy its basic assumptions, possibly in order to reform the government it, itself, created. The opposition needs to establish its unity on something more substantial than negativism. The instability of the political-party system has contributed to the strength of pressure groups, which have been able to promote special interests to the detriment of the individual voter. *Ticos* are free to make changes on election day, but what happens between elections is usually out of their control. Such a situation has not caused serious problems so far, because Costa Rican governments in recent times have represented the popular will. When the government fails to do so, *tico* democracy will be put to a severe test.

The democracy that Costa Rica has enjoyed has also brought it international prestige. Although not a powerful country, Costa Rica has earned respect abroad. It is frequently said that a nation's foreign policy reflects its domestic character, and Costa Rica seems to fit this pattern. At times, though, being a democracy in the Central American and Caribbean area has not been easy.

5

FOREIGN RELATIONS

Until 1950, Costa Rican foreign relations were guided by two principal factors: geographic isolation and the peaceful disposition of the people. Formidable natural barriers and meager resources confined the *ticos* to the Meseta Central and, at the same time, kept outsiders away. During the colonial period, the center of Spanish control, in Guatemala, was too remote to influence Costa Rican affairs, and *ticos* themselves showed faint interest in the overall governance of the isthmus. Local crown officials were left to govern as well as they could, providing little revenue to the metropolis and receiving little in return. After independence, and during the Central American federation period (1823-39), Costa Rica played only a nominal role in the government of the union, refusing to get involved in the internecine strife that marked the era. After its separation from the federation, Costa Rica remained aloof from isthmian affairs and pursued its own destiny. It did not encourage efforts to restore the union and resisted the attempts by strongmen Justo Rufino Barrios, in Guatemala (in the 1870s) and José Santos Zelaya, in Nicaragua (at the turn of the century), to reunify the isthmus by force of arms.

Four centuries of virtual isolation produced a strong sense of provincialism among the *ticos*. They felt that they were different from their isthmian cousins. Principally, they did not have the "Indian problem", neither politically nor ethnically, that they ascribed to the turbulent political conditions of their northern neighbors. This sense of superiority did not engender the ambition to assert leadership and straighten out isthmian affairs, but, rather, reinforced the attitude of withdrawal and the wish to insulate the nation against conditions viewed as alien. A common witticism stated that all roads in Costa Rica were good, except those leading to Nicaragua, in order to keep the Nicaraguans out. The *ticos* were not without compassion for the problems of their neighbors, but believed that the best policy was to set an example of peace and order, which the other Central American states might follow. Costa Rica was very concerned with its image internationally and strove to be looked upon favorably. Beyond this, Costa Rica attempted to maintain neutrality in Central American affairs and to be a moral force, while, at the same time, providing a haven for refugees from tyranny and for political exiles.

To be sure, Costa Rica had its times of international strife. It could not always protect its frontiers against the turmoil of its neighbors. The activities of the adventurer William Walker in the 1850s in Nicaragua and Honduras spilled over into Costa Rica, and the *ticos* raised an army to resist the invader, who was repelled in Costa Rica's finest hour. The presence of political exiles in Costa Rica occasionally created problems and involved Costa Rica in the filibustering activities common to the region. In fact, the *tico* Jorge Volio was himself a notorious filibusterer, who used Nicaraguan soil for launching his attack against the dictator Federico Tinoco in 1919. Boundary disputes also interrupted the peaceful policy of Costa Rica, and until such issues were resolved in the 1930s, relations with Nicaragua and Panama were strained. However, Costa Rica showed a disposition to settle these matters by arbitration rather than by force of arms. Throughout its history, Costa Rica has been a strong advocate of the pacific settlement of disputes and has participated in international conventions and organizations established for that purpose.

In its international relations outside the Central American region, Costa Rica has been guided largely by economic considerations. First England, then Germany, and, finally, the United States have been its major trading partners. Once Costa Rica entered the coffee era, the price of coffee became its principal proccupation, and it has sought to maintain a stable price and steady market. Costa Rica's relations with the United States generally have been warm and cordial. Costa Rica was a U.S. ally in both world wars and it has consistently supported North American initiatives in hemispheric and world affairs. Its criticism of U.S. interventionism during the early decades of this century was mild in comparison with that of the other nations of Central America and the Caribbean. When the United States intervened in Nicaragua in the 1920s, although Costa Rica's position was discreetly neutral, Ricardo Jiménez secretly supported the intervention in the belief that it would restore stability to the region. Costa Rica was no puppet of the United States, but it was the least troublesome of the Latin American states, and, when the United States embraced the principles of nonintervention and representative democracy in the Good Neighbor era, Costa Rica welcomed U.S. leadership in inter-American affairs. This placid and passive position ended abruptly in the aftermath of the 1948 civil war.

Support for democracy was a natural corollary to the basic tenets of Costa Rican foreign policy, given Costa Rica's domestic character, but the circumstances surrounding the 1948 armed struggle transformed this position into aggressive, antidicta-torial action. José Figueres, in planning the 1948 uprising, had sought the assistance of various exile groups of the Caribbean and Central America. As previously noted, he entered into the Pact of the Caribbean in Guatemala in December 1947, in which he pledged to assist these exiles in liberating their homelands, if they would help him against Rafael Calderón. Once Figueres had defeated Calderón, with the assistance of the exile groups and their supplies of arms, Costa Rica became the base for the so-called Caribbean Legion. Although Figueres had made the pact as a private citizen, as president of the founding junta, he, in effect, subordinated Costa Rican foreign policy to the general purposes of the exile commanders. He had promised to permit the use of Costa Rican soil for the preparation of revolutionary actions against dictatorships in Nicaragua, Honduras, and the Dominican Republic.

Relations between Costa Rica and Nicaragua had long been strained, but under Figueres they deteriorated rapidly. A primary target of the Pact of the Caribbean was the Nicaraguan dictator

Anastasio Somoza Garcia, and Nicaraguan exiles, along with other nationalities in the revolutionary camp, began training in 1948 for an armed expedition. Figueres (Don Pepe) provided the Caribbean Legion with money, arms, and encampments, but the responsibilities of his office, plus the fact that Somoza probably had the best army in Central America, tended to cool his ardor. He was entrapped by his own rashness, but, fortunately for him, he was able to renege on his pledge without appearing to do so, owing to dissensions within the exile groups themselves. Figueres kept postponing the zero hour and let things drift. At the same time, in an apparent contradiction of his aggressive policy, Don Pepe abolished the Costa Rican army in December 1948. However, if Figueres was having second thoughts, Somoza was already provoked.

Somoza had been extremely upset over Figueres's victory in the 1948 civil war, as well as over the company he kept. Somoza gave refuge to Calderón and Teodoro Picado and encouraged them to make plans for an armed action of their own. Somoza was aware of events in Costa Rica, because he had placed spies in the training camps of the Caribbean Legion, and, even if Figueres procrastinated, Somoza had no intention of permitting his enemies to surprise him. With Somoza's support, a small band of Calderonistas invaded the northwest corner of Guanacaste province in late December 1948. With no army to defend Costa Rica, and with no wish to use the Caribbean Legion and thereby provide Somoza with an excuse to enter the conflict, Don Pepe invoked the Inter-American Treaty of Reciprocal Assistance (the Rio Treaty) and called upon the Organization of American States (OAS) to end the conflict. Within hours, the OAS requested a cease-fire and called upon both Costa Rica and Nicaragua to honor their inter-American commitments. The action of the OAS put an end to the invasion, but Figueres had been chastened, and the Caribbean Legion was ordered to leave Costa Rica.

This episode served to involve Costa Rica deeply in the anti-dictatorial struggle in the Caribbean. The Caribbean Legion moved to Guatemala, where it fared no better, undertaking an unsuccessful invasion of the Dominican Republic in June 1949. The following year, the United States, anxious to maintain stability in the Caribbean region, in the context of the cold war, put an end to filibustering activity. It enjoined the Caribbean states from sponsoring exile revolutionary movements and encouraged them to maintain normal diplomatic relations in order to ease tensions. However, military dictatorships were on the rise, and by 1952, Costa Rica was the only democratic state in the Caribbean, other than Mexico and Puerto Rico.

When Figueres became constitutional president in 1953, hundreds of exiles fleeing the dictators sought refuge in Costa Rica. They came to Figueres for help not merely because of Costa Rica's tradition of providing a haven, but also because Don Pepe had become a leader of the democratic left in Latin America. This movement endeavored to provide an option to right-wing dictators and left-wing extremists. Foremost among the exiles was Rómulo Betancourt, the former president of Venezuela and the leader of the Democratic Action Party (AD). At the time, Venezuela was under the rule of a dictator, Colonel Marcos Pérez Jiménez, and Figueres provided Betancourt with facilities on his *finca*, La Lucha, for a clandestine radio transmitter for communicating with the AD underground inside Venezuela. Betancourt was also engaged in a campaign to persuade Latin American countries to boycott the Tenth Inter-American Conference, scheduled to meet in Caracas in early 1954. Although Betancourt was received sympathetically in the democratic states of Chile and Uruguay, in the end, only Figueres's Costa Rica refused to attend the conference. Pérez Jiménez was angered, but the United States also resented the action, because U.S. Secretary of State John Foster Dulles used the conference to try to rally inter-American opinion against the allegedly Communist government of Jacobo Arbenz in Guatemala. Figueres was firmly pro-United States, particularly in the prevailing East-West conflict, but he criticized Dulles's policy as sterile, because it favored stability in the hemisphere as a means of combating communism. Figueres felt it had the effect of supporting military dictatorships and that it failed to confront communism in the only effective way, by overcoming social injustice and promoting economic development. As the spokesman for this position, Figueres earned an international reputation, but it also compounded his difficulties with his neighbor, Somoza.

Despite his close call in 1948, Figueres continued to support Nicaraguan exiles in opposition to Somoza. In April 1954, this took the form of an assassination attempt, in which a small band of exiles infiltrated Nicaragua from Costa Rica, after being transported to the frontier in vehicles belonging to Figueres and being escorted by officers of the Civil Guard of Costa Rica. Somoza captured the would-be assassins and extracted their confessions, becoming incensed when he learned about Figueres's complicity. He decided to aid Calderón and Picado in yet another invasion of Costa Rica. This time, Pérez-Jiménez contributed money and arms, and the Dominican dictator, Rafael Trujillo, who had been an earlier target of the Caribbean Legion, also pledged assistance.

In January 1955, Calderón's forces attacked from a base within Nicaragua and penetrated a few miles into Costa Rica. Don Pepe rallied a small force of volunteers and appealed to the OAS to stop the invasion. The OAS called upon Nicaragua and Costa Rica to refrain from further belligerency, and sent an investigating committee to the isthmus. The presence of the OAS committee stopped the hostilities at the front, but the invaders had a small air force, including an F-47 Thunderbolt fighter, that strafed a number of Costa Rican towns. Costa Rica, lacking modern equipment for its defense, petitioned the OAS to supply it with fighter planes and antiaircraft guns. With the approval of the OAS, the United States sold Costa Rica four F-51 Mustang fighters at a dollar apiece, which brought the affair to an abrupt halt.

The OAS had rescued Figueres again, but the United States warned him that he had to stop his conspiratorial activities. The U.S. assistant secretary of state for inter-American affairs, Henry F. Holland, referred to Figueres as "a troublemaker" (Ameringer, 1974), and the U.S. Department of State virtually forced Betancourt to leave San José and relocate in Puerto Rico, where he could be watched more closely. Despite its displeasure, the State Department had saved Don Pepe, owing to pressure from leading North American liberals, including Senator Paul Douglas of Illinois, who argued that the dictators had ganged up on the only democrat in the region. Don Pepe's policy had brought Costa Rica close to disaster, but the support he enjoyed in democratic circles in the hemisphere enhanced the reputation of the small nation. Although these activities took their toll in Costa Rican lives and caused economic hardship, Costa Rica had assumed a leadership role in hemispheric affairs that was far beyond what its size and resources would seem to command. Nonetheless, under the watchful eye of the OAS,

Nicaragua and Costa Rica entered into a series of agreements in which they pledged to resolve all future disputes peacefully. Somoza was subsequently assassinated in September 1956, but Figueres was not involved in any way.

Figueres was in Italy at the time, as part of a trip to Western Europe in search of markets for coffee and expanded channels of trade. Figueres had criticized U.S. policy in Latin America not only for its apparent tolerance of dictators, but also for its neglect of economic and social problems. Figueres believed that the poor countries of Latin America, dependent upon a few agricultural products or minerals, were at a disadvantage in dealing with the industrialized nations, such as the United States. Failing to persuade the United States to undertake a program of economic assistance in Latin America, or to pay higher prices for its products, Figueres traveled to Western Europe to try to improve Costa Rica's competitive position by offering to purchase manufactured goods from any country that would give Costa Rica better prices for its coffee and bananas. He visited England, Denmark, West Germany, France, and Italy, but only in the latter country did he actually negotiate a commercial transaction, acquiring an automatic telephone system in exchange for Costa Rican products. Although Figueres failed to relieve Costa Rica of its economic dependence upon the United States, or to find a solution to Costa Rica's chronic problem of fluctuating coffee prices, his efforts to interest the United States in Latin America's economic problems suddenly paid off.

The rise of Castro in Cuba indeed convinced the United States that it might have been wrong in neglecting Latin America's economic and social problems and in failing to support the democratic reformers. Although he was no longer in office in 1959, Figueres continued to influence Costa Rican foreign relations through his leadership in the PLN and his position as a spokesman for Latin America's non-Communist left. During the time that Castro had been fighting the dictator Fulgencio Batista, Figueres aided Castro with arms and money, and Cubans used Costa Rican territory to support their guerrilla operations. After his victory, Castro invited Figueres to Havana in April 1959 to thank him personally for his help. Figueres delivered an address before the Cuban Workers Confederation, in which he praised the Cuban revolution but advised

Castro not to undermine the solidarity of the West. Castro retorted that Cuba would be neutral in East-West relations and attacked Figueres as a "bad friend" and a "bad revolutionary" (New York *Times*, April 4, 1959). Following this break, the United States, through the Central Intelligence Agency, offered to assist Figueres and the social-democratic movements of Latin America in promoting democratic reform, as a means of preventing the spread of Castroism. With covert funding from the CIA, Don Pepe and other leaders of the democratic left, including Betancourt (again the president of Venezuela), established the Inter-American Institute of Political Education in San José. The purpose of the institute was to analyze Latin America's economic and social problems and to train young leaders of allied political parties throughout the hemisphere in political organization and strategy. In many respects, the Costa Rican model for economic and social reform within a democratic framework was being presented as an alternative to the radical modes of the Cuban revolution.

In the meantime, Figueres also supported more violent forms of competition with Castro. During the summer of 1959, Castro assisted a number of revolutionary actions against the remaining dictators of the Caribbean. Fearing that a Castro-sponsored movement might succeed in Nicaragua, Don Pepe helped a group of Nicaraguan exiles to prepare an attack upon the Somoza dynasty. Don Pepe furnished the Nicaraguans, (under the leadership of the democrat Pedro Joaquín Chamorro), with a training base at Punta Llorona, in the south of Costa Rica, and at the end of May 1959, helped to airlift approximately 160 guerrillas into Nicaragua. This time, Nicaragua appealed to the OAS, declaring that it was a victim of aggression; and the OAS, acting with less alacrity than on the occasions of Don Pepe's problems, sent a committee to Costa Rica and Nicaragua to investigate the charge. The affair was embarrassing to Costa Rican President Mario Echandi, who declared officially that Costa Rica was neutral, but who realized that the action was popular among the *ticos* and that he could not move too vigorously against Figueres and the PLN. In the end, he was saved from further embarrassment, because the guerrilla movement collapsed within Nicaragua itself, but the affair illustrated that, even with the opposition in power, Figueres and the PLN continued to involve Costa Rica in the antidictatorial struggle.

This involvement took a number of forms. In mid-1960, the OAS selected San José as the site for two meetings of consultation. The first dealt with the attempt by the Dominican dictator Trujillo to assassinate Venezuelan President Betancourt, and with Venezuela's demand for the imposition of sanctions against the Dominican Republic. The second, held immediately afterward, involved complaints by Peru and the United States that Cuba had fallen under the influence of an extracontinental power, the Soviet Union, and that such influence constituted a threat to the peace and security of the hemisphere. The selection of San José for these meetings indicated the respect that the OAS held for the stability and maturity of Costa Rica. When the Kennedy administration came to power in 1961, Figueres's campaign for a program of U.S. economic assistance for Latin America bore fruit with the Alliance for Progress. Don Pepe was on intimate terms with a number of President Kennedy's top advisors, principally Adolf Berle, who consulted Figueres frequently in drawing up and implementing plans for the *Alianza*. President Kennedy himself visited Costa Rica in 1963 to attend the meeting of the chiefs of state of Central America.

Despite his close ties with the Kennedy White House, Figueres was not involved in the Bay of Pigs affair, and Costa Rica played no part. In fact, Figueres was opposed to the attack on Castro unless the United States would prove its sincerity in the struggle against dictators by first getting rid of the right-wing tyrant Trujillo. To this end, he cooperated with Cord Meyer, a high-ranking CIA officer, in an attempt to organize Dominican exiles in a movement against Trujillo. Even after the failure of the Bay of Pigs, he convened a secret meeting at La Lucha in May 1961, composed of Dominican exile leaders Juan Bosch and Horacio Ornes and of U.S., Costa Rican, Puerto Rican, and Venezuelan sponsors, for the purpose of creating a coalition government in anticipation of the fall of Trujillo. The plan was aborted at the end of the same month, when Trujillo was assassinated in an unrelated plot. However, Bosch eventually became president of the Dominican Republic. Because of their relationship, Figueres's influence in the hemisphere diminished following the death of President Kennedy in November 1963, and Costa Rica's foreign policy for the remainder of the sixties and during the seventies was one more of peace and less of conspiracy. The Institute for Political Education also fell on hard times, with the revelations in *Ramparts* magazine, in February 1967, of the CIA's covert funding of such organizations. The Ebert Foundation of West Germany subsequently became its sponsor and linked it with the European social-democratic movement, but Don Pepe's role was reduced. Economic problems returned as the main concern of foreign relations.

The gradual abandonment of the Alliance for Progress, and the economic losses accompanying the Irazú volcanic eruption in 1963, placed heavy strains upon Costa Rica's economy. The Johnson administration attempted a new approach to Latin America's economic problems, through the promotion of regional trading blocs and agreements. In Central America, this took the form of the Central American Common Market, designed to stimulate development by means of an expanded market for encouraging investment and industrialization. The idea of Central American economic integration has always had an appeal as a substitute for the failure to achieve political union, but Costa Rica has been a reluctant participant. It suspected that its higher wages and larger commitment to social programs would place it at a disadvantage with the other states, where wages were low and social overhead virtually non-existent. Its concern appears to have been justified, and Costa Rica has complained that the costs and benefits of economic integration have not been shared equally. Costa Rica has experienced increased industrialization, but only because it subsidized it heavily, and Costa Rica has been inundated by cheap consumer products from its neighbors. Generally, the political problems in the region have hindered the development of the Common Market, and Costa Rica has done little to try to solve these problems, almost as if it welcomed them as a convenient excuse for its own foot-dragging. Economic integration has, in fact, increased tensions in the region, rather than soothing them.

When Figueres became president again in 1970, although he did not abandon the Common Market, he renewed the search for alternative markets for Costa Rica's agricultural products and for better and more stable prices for its goods. Figueres realized that the Central American states essentially produced the same commodities and that, instead of trading among themselves,they ought to try to cooperate in the marketing and pricing of their goods outside the region. In an effort similar to the Organization of Petroleum Exporting Countries (OPEC), Figueres attempted to organize the banana-producing countries, proposing a $1 export tax upon every box of bananas shipped. The plan had little success, because as I heard *ticos* themselves joke: "Cars don't run on bananas." In a more controversial move, Figueres undertook to negotiate trade agreements with the Soviet Union and other Communist-bloc countries. For this purpose, Don Pepe established diplomatic relations with the USSR toward the end of 1970. This action led to numerous protest demonstrations, and the right-wing Costa Rica Libre (MCRL) even started training paramilitary units for a possible coup attempt. Although Figueres ridiculed these protests with the observation that Russian tractors did not come with the "bacillus of communism" (Ameringer, 1979), there was a moment of excitement in February 1971, when a rather half-hearted coup was quickly suppressed. At the time, Don Pepe was actually visiting Disney World in Florida with his children. The establishment of relations with the Soviet Union did not result in significant trade, but the United States viewed the Soviet embassy in San José with misgivings because of its potential for subversion in Central America.

Figueres's second presidency (1970-74) was not as turbulent in the international sphere as was his first tenure during the fifties. In fact, Figueres conferred on a number of occasions with Nicaragua's President Anastasio Somoza Debayle (the son of his former enemy). They met in June 1971 in an effort to mediate the troubles between El Salvador and Honduras — the so-called Soccer War — in order to revive the Common Market. Later, Figueres visited Somoza following the Managua earthquake of December 1972, to discuss the plight of thousands of Nicaraguans who had fled to Costa Rica in terror and were living in a makeshift refugee camp near Liberia. As Figueres said, "We are not conspiring against the son." (Ameringer, 1979) Exiles continued to seek refuge in Costa Rica, but Figueres was not supporting filibustering expeditions at the time. His most troublesome refugee was the fugitive financier Vesco, whom Figueres welcomed to Costa Rica in the hope that he would invest in the country and encourage others to do so. Figueres proposed a plan to establish an international banking zone in Costa Rica, similar to that of Switzerland and of the Bahamas; but he abandoned the idea in the wake of the scandal surrounding the source of Vesco's $224-million fortune, and his own personal financial dealings with Vesco.

Every effort that Figueres made to improve Costa Rica's international trade seemed to result in controversy. *Ticos* severely criticized Figueres and his foreign minister, Gonzalo Facio, for Costa Rica's extensive involvement in international organizatons, which required the funding of numerous delegations and a great deal of foreign travel. Figueres argued that Costa Rica could not improve its economic status or upgrade its technology without such participation, but *ticos*, traditionally stay-at-homes, looked upon this activity as pretentious and as junketeering. The seventies were a period of austerity, with falling coffee prices and rising fuel costs, and Figueres could not restore Costa Rica to its former position as a democratic leader of the hemisphere. Even Don Pepe's claim that the then Venezuelan President Carlos Andrés Pérez, who had been an exile in Costa Rica in the fifties, would "not let Costa Rica go without oil" (Ameringer, 1979) did not convince *ticos* that his active foreign policy was worth the price. Almost to the end of the decade, foreign relations took a backseat to domestic problems.

The outbreak of civil war in Nicaragua in 1978 shook the complacency of the *ticos*. Following the Managua earthquake, the political situation in Nicaragua had begun to deteriorate. Somoza engaged in shameless profiteering in carrying out the process of earthquake relief and reconstruction and became repressive when opposition leaders exposed his conduct. By the time Jimmy Carter became president of the United States in 1977, the human rights performance of Somoza was a very bad one. Carter, making human rights the centerpiece of his foreign policy, criticized the Somoza government and withheld the military and economic assistance that Nicaragua had been receiving almost routinely. These actions encouraged the opponents of the Somoza dynasty, but the Sandinista National Liberation Front (FSLN), a hitherto small revolutionary organization backed principally by Castro, seized the initiative. In a series of dramatic episodes, especially the occupation of the National Palace in Managua and the holding of 1,500 hostages, including the entire Nicaraguan Congress, the Sandinistas forged to the front of the anti-Somoza movement.

Within Costa Rica, hundreds of Nicaraguan exiles became active in the movement and openly used Costa Rican soil for their operations. They enjoyed the sympathy of the PLN, particularly the social-democratic elements, and President Rodrigo Carazo, a former Liberacionista and a critic of Somoza, did not interfere with their activities. Carazo and the PLN were deeply concerned about the fate of Nicaragua, and, although they aided the Sandinistas, their main purpose was to assure a role for the moderate, democratic elements in the future government of Nicaragua. At the time of Somoza's fall in July 1979, Nicaraguan guerrilla forces were launching attacks on Nicaragua from sanctuaries within Costa Rica, and arms flowed freely to the rebels via Costa Rica from sources in Panama, Cuba, Venezuela, and elsewhere. These arms sales themselves became a source of controversy and scandal, because of charges, still unproved, that Carazo accepted as much as $30 million in bribes in relation to the gunrunning activities. It has also been suggested that Carazo supported the fighting in Nicaragua, in order to divert attention from his problems at home. In the end, Costa Rica's gamble did not pay off, because the Sandinistas became the dominant force in Nicaragua, and Cuba, not the Christian- and social-democratic movements of Costa Rica and Venezuela, emerged as the most influential foreign element in Nicaragua.

The presence of a radical, revolutionary regime in Nicaragua is the latest serious problem for Costa Rica in the area of foreign relations. Although democratic forces are still competing in Nicaragua, and the United States, during 1980, attempted to support them and the development of a pluralistic society, the decision of the Reagan administration to cut off economic assistance to Nicaragua may prove to strengthen the position of the hard-liners in the Nicaraguan revolution. The outbreak of violence in El Salvador and the increasingly serious political situation in Guatemala have brought a new wave of political exiles to Costa Rica, many of them highly radicalized. In the past, with the exceptions already noted, Costa Rica has tried to curb the political activities of such exiles, but these new elements have been more militant and less considerate of their *tico* hosts. Moreover, Costa Rica's own unemployment problems are making it difficult to absorb this influx of exiles, and even intellectuals, who once had no difficulty in finding teaching positions, are without work. There have also been several terrorist episodes in Costa Rica since mid-1980, the most serious occurring in March 1981 in the form of a grenade attack upon a van transporting U.S. Marine embassy guards. The following month, in an unprecedented move, the Carazo government raided the headquarters of a Guatemalan exile group and expelled approximately 40 of its members for subversive activities. *Ticos* fear, for the first time, that Costa Rica is becoming "Central Americanized."Although the weakness of its military and security forces renders it vulnerable, Costa Rica's peaceful image may protect it from the turbulence of the isthmian region.

This image was enhanced by the decision to open an international University for Peace in Costa Rica in 1982. Carazo made the proposal before the UN General Assembly in 1978. The United Nations endorsed the idea, but did not commit any funds, and the university will depend upon the willing support of governments and private organizations. Costa Rica has provided land for the campus and has devised a plan, in cooperation with other Central American and Caribbean states, to levy 10¢ on each imported barrel of oil needed for the operation of the school. There is general agreement that Costa Rica is an appropriate site for the study of the issue of peace. Despite a revolution next door and deteriorating political conditions in Central America, the threat to Costa Rica's reputation for being peaceful is more internal than external, as *tico* democracy must face serious domestic problems in the 1980s.

6

THE PROBLEMS OF TICO DEMOCRACY

The most persistent criticism of *tico* democracy is that the welfare state has grown beyond the capacity of the Costa Rican economy to support it and that the system has become institutionalized and resistant to reform. Analysts, such as Charles Denton (1971), claim that the Costa Rican political system is too democratic, that there are more checks than balances, and that the system has become "immobilized." The existing Costa Rican socio-politico-economic system has been evolving for 30 years, but it has been a piecemeal development, responding to needs as they arose, rather than overall planning; and it appears that the time is approaching for taking stock. The main trouble is that the system has produced a new middle class, a bureaucratic bourgeoisie, that has an obvious interest in the system and has acquired the political strength to defend it. There is no question that Costa Rica has made great strides in providing its people with social justice and economic opportunity, but it has been spending more than it earns and it cannot go on running budget deficits endlessly. The problem is more economic than ideological, because if coffee and bananas produced as much revenue as petroleum, there is little doubt that the Costa Rican system would be among the most equitable in the world, in terms of passing the benefits along to the people.

The paradox is that Costa Rica's advanced social system and the well-being of its middle class are based upon a primitive economic structure dependent upon two principal agricultural products. In fact, coffee and bananas account for over one-half of Costa Rica's foreign earnings, with which it must purchase most manufactured items, all capital goods and hydrocarbon fuels, and a surprisingly large amount of foodstuffs. When the prices of coffee and bananas are high, as they were in 1975 when Brazil suffered a devastating frost, the Costa Rican economy prospers. However, in recent years the prices have been steadily declining, and Costa Rica's economy is in a crisis. In 1980, coffee earnings dropped by 22 percent, whereas the cost of oil imports increased by 28 percent (see Tables 4 and 5). The result was a $670-million balance-of-payments deficit, and inflation during 1981 reached an annual rate of 40 percent. Thirty percent of Costa Rica's export earnings is used to service the foreign debt. Although President Carazo devalued the *colón* by one-half early in 1981, the economic growth rate for 1981 was expected to be only 1 percent, in contrast to an average of 6 percent in recent years. Unemployment stands at 15 percent and it is increasing. All of these indicators demonstrate that Costa Rica has been living beyond its means, but the prescribed austerity measures and budget cuts are difficult to undertake because of the political power of the bureaucracy.

Approximately 130,000 persons are employed by one form of government entity or another. They comprise about 20 percent of the total work force and absorb 28 percent of the national income. The public sector has provided most of the new jobs in the last two decades. In addition to the normal public-service functions, agencies of the Costa Rican government include business enterprises and utilities, regulatory bodies, and social-service institutions. Nonetheless, since it primarily performs services, the public sector has contributed to the decline in productivity, when measured by goods produced and the number of persons employed. Although one hears comments about a "swollen" bureaucracy, most responsible observers do not criticize the size of the bureaucracy per se, given the high growth rate of the Costa Rican population and the nation's commitment to social programs. They complain instead about the

TABLE 4
The Role of Coffee Exports in the Costa Rican Economy

Harvest Year, April 1-March 31	Volume (in metric tons)	Price per Kg ($U.S., FOB)	Total Value ($U.S., FOB in thousands)	Percent of Total Exports
1970-71	66,537.08	0.91	60,384	—
1971-72	83,423.62	0.88	73,723	—
1972-73	70,789.37	1.27	89,984	—
1973-74	86,104.44	1.40	120,278	—
1974-75	74,982.54	1.15	85,886	—
1975-76	69,797.20	2.03	141,679	25.96
1976-77	67,197.38	4.38	294,154	38.54
1977-78	78,458.25	3.52	276,237	36.27
1978-79	91,741.26	2.70	247,397	33.81
1979-80	79,170.73	3.37	266,657	24.21
1980-81	106,004.73	2.28	241,945	22.90

Source: Oficina del Café, *Informe sobre la actividad cafetalera de Costa Rica* (San José, 1981).

95

TABLE 5
The Role of Petroleum Imports

Year	Price per Barrel (42 Gallons, $U.S.)			Total Value ($U.S., in thousands)	Percent of Total Imports
	Crude	Diesel	Gasoline		
1973	4.88	7.06	7.17	28,189	6.2
1976	12.81	13.93	15.75	61,479	9.0
1979	19.76	29.83	32.94	168,887	11.9
1980	—	—	—	216,175	—

Source: OFIPLAN, *Plan Nacional de Desarrollo, 1979-1982* (San José, 1980).

bureaucracy's appropriation of a larger share of the national budget for its own salaries and benefits, charging that the public-service employees take too much for themselves and leave too little for providing services for the poor and society at large. Public employees are the best-organized workers in Costa Rica and they have conducted strikes for better wages and working conditions, causing a steady climb in the cost of government. Their ability to paralyze government and their effective action as a pressure group make it extremely difficult to institute reforms that might be in the best interests of society but would require the bureaucracy to make sacrifices. The so-called bureaucratic bourgeoisie is accused of being insensitive to the needs of the poor.

This new middle class, which provides strength for *tico* democracy, also contains the potential for its destruction, if it continues to think only about itself and neglects the very basis for its being. As the bureaucracy grew, it was only natural that it would recruit the best-educated citizens; but the PLN apparently used the bureaucracy as an escape valve for the unemployment problem, responding particularly to the search by university graduates and intellectuals for jobs and diverting them, in the process, from radical political activity. The Costa Rican educational system, widely praised for elevating the literacy and civic consciousness of *ticos*, emphasizes humanistic studies and social sciences; so, in the midst of a shortage of clerical and technical workers, there is a surplus of white-collar personnel, and the bureaucracy almost of necessity was expanded to absorb them. Moreover, the benefits these workers receive have tended to become a standard for white-collar personnel in the private sector, adding to the burdens placed upon the economy. When government employees received the *aguinaldo* (actually, a thirteenth month of pay as a Christmas bonus), workers throughout the entire urban economy demanded the same. There is also a great deal of downtime in the bureaucracy because of the large number of holidays and *fiestas*. There are approximately 15 national holidays, which government employees receive with pay, along with 15 days of annual paid vacation, amounting to what the Biesanzes (1979) have described as "institutionalized vagrancy." Stone (1975) has deplored the attitude of the public-sector employees in looking upon government as "a vast cornucopia." Efforts to overcome this attitude are frustrated by the autonomy enjoyed by the state institutions themselves, the effective unionization of the public-sector employees, and the protection provided by the civil-service system.

As already noted, Costa Rica has one of the best civil-service systems in Latin America, from the standpoint of its independence from the politicians. Although there are complaints that the selection system is far from perfect or fair, there are, nonetheless, no mass firings when a change of government takes place, and the spoils system is defunct in Costa Rica. On the other hand, new administrations frequently have created new layers of jobs to take care of their supporters, while retaining the old. Workers cannot be fired for political reasons, and it is difficult to remove them for other reasons (even legitimate) as well. Unfortunately, job security has not resulted in greater efficiency. The civil-service system (including the distinct plans governing the employment of persons in the autonomous institutions) attempts to be fair through uniform pay scales and job classification, but the system rewards longevity rather than merit. Raises and promotions are based upon seniority rather than ability or proven competence. Although these are basically public-administration problems and the benefits of the system outweigh the disadvantages, the image of the public-sector employee as untouchable is another factor in the erosion of public confidence in the bureaucracy. Public employees are looked upon as well paid, insolent, and indolent. Partly, the problem is a cultural one, as *ticos* are social persons and resent the impersonality and long waiting lines of the bureaucratic apparatus. Hints of favoritism and corruption in the system further undermine the situation. When the economy was expanding, *ticos* appeared to tolerate these abuses, but now, as the economy slows down and approaches a crisis, the resistance of the bureaucracy to change or reform and the continued neglect of the needs of the poor can only lead to social unrest.

The problem of the bureaucratic bourgeoisie is closely related to that of another new element of the middle class, the so-called managerial class. Although Costa Rica was lukewarm to the Central American Common Market, it recognized the opportunity for stimulating industrialization. Even before 1960, the PLN had favored industrial growth as a possible answer to Costa Rica's dependence upon agricultural production. In the scheme of the Common Market, *tico* planners saw the opportunity for industry in a regional market that a national market alone could not support. They figured that, although Costa Rican wage scales were higher than those of the other Central American states, foreign investors would be more willing to establish factories in Costa Rica because of the high educational level of *ticos* and the stable political conditions. To this end, the Costa Rican government encouraged foreign entrepreneurs, especially North Americans, to build their plants in Costa Rica, by offering them tariff protection, tax exemptions, and subsidies through the national banking system, plus land and public services. During the sixties and seventies, the industrial sector was one of the fastest-growing elements of the economy, accounting for 4 percent of total exports in 1960 and growing to 30 percent in 1978. During the same period, the number of persons employed by industry rose from 43,000 to 104,000. Nonetheless, despite this growth, the *ticos* discovered that it was costing them more in incentives and subsidies than they were receiving in return. The new industry was engaged in import substitution and the production of items for mass consumption, but protectionism dictated high prices (adding to the burden of the agricultural sector), and profits were siphoned off by the owners in the United States and elsewhere. By the time the *ticos* became aware of the problem they had created, they had to deal with a local managerial class, which used its political influence to defend the privileged position of its foreign bosses.

The new managerial class, composed of many Liberacionista

politicians, who got in on the ground floor, is looked upon with a great deal of suspicion in Costa Rica. It is described as a Trojan horse, doing the bidding of foreign economic interests. Stone (1975) relates that many of these managers were recruited from the *conquistador* class; they have the *sangre,* and they give the foreign enterprises what they want: family ties with the elite, political influence, and technical competence. He argues that this connection actually perpetuates underdevelopment, because, while the managers run the plants, the key economic decisions are made in foreign boardrooms. The managers, who have a stake because of their well-paid jobs, must defend these decisions, whether they are in the best interests of Costa Rica or not. This is the dependency theory, but many *tico* scholars are convinced that it has validity. More-over, these critics are not all on the left. In fact, the Carazo admin-istration, in its *National Plan for Development, 1979-82,* is very critical of the industrial sector and feels strongly that, if it cannot survive without the help of the Costa Rican government, it ought to be abandoned. The Biesanzes (1979), on the other hand, feel that the *ticos* are partially to blame for this state of affairs because of their failure to "think big." They criticize the *ticos* for refusing to invest in industry — in corporate business — and for creating a vacuum, which foreign entrepreneurs came in to fill. In all these problems relating to the economy, particularly the role of the state, whether through direct intervention or through various in-centives, one needs to consider that the public sector did not replace private enterprise, but that it acted where the private sector did not exist. Nonetheless, the Carazo administration feels that it is wrong to continue to commit resources to industry, which it regards as inefficient and as contributing to inflation, while Costa Rican agriculture stagnates.

Agriculture remains the principal element of the Costa Rican economy, upon which rest the bureaucratic bourgeoisie and the new managerial class, the present beneficiaries of the system. The future of *tico* democracy may indeed depend upon the health of the agrarian sector. Alberto Cañas (1978) has said that the small proprietor was once the backbone of *tico* democracy, but the yeoman farmer of Costa Rica hardly exists anymore. The problem of land distribution is not as acute in Costa Rica as in other Latin American countries, but the concentration of land in the hands of a relatively few owners is more serious than the myth of Costa Rica admits. Moreover, the increase in the size of landholdings appears to be continuing, according to the most recent data: the farm and ranch census for 1963 and for 1973. In 1963, 6.5 percent of all *fincas* were 100 hectares or more in size (one hectare equals 2.47 acres) and they comprised 62.4 percent of all agricultural land, whereas in 1973, 7.3 percent of all *fincas* had 100 hectares or more and they occupied 67 percent of the farmland. Actually, in the latter year, only 1 percent of the *fincas* had over 500 hectares, but they took up 36 percent of the land. On the other hand, in 1973, 45.8 percent of all *fincas* had less than five hectares and they contained only 1.9 percent of the agricultural land. Admittedly, by Latin American standards, Costa Rica had a substantial number of medium-sized holdings in 1973 — those from five to 100 hectares, which made up 46.9 percent of all *fincas* and held 31.1 percent of the land fit for cultivation. However, a more critical and current figure (1980) is that approximately three-quarters of all rural workers are landless peasants.

The factors explaining the engrossment of landholdings and the decline of the peasantry are the increased mechanization of farming and the growth in the number of cattle ranches, especially in Guanacaste. In an effort to keep up with the costs of industrialization and the growing social overhead, agriculture tried to be more efficient and to produce more. However, in many respects, it only saw its economic strength reduced, because of the near saturation of the international market for its products and the accompanying fall in prices. While small peasant holders lost their lands to agribusiness, mechanization and grazing also reduced the need for farm laborers. Whereas agriculture employed 49.7 percent of the total work force in 1963, it employed only 30.4 percent in 1978. Despite the fact that employment in industry increased from 11.7 percent to 15.2 percent of the total labor force during the same period, it was not enough to absorb the available workers, and unemployment and underemployment resulted. The policies of the government in diverting resources to the public sector and to industry only added to rural misery. Moreover, the coffee barons have not helped to alleviate the situation. They have been very conservative in their investments, staying with the known quantity, coffee, and refusing to experiment in new agricultural products, such as foodstuffs, which the expanding urban sectors need. Even when the oligarchs sold their lands, making room for the urbanization of the Meseta Central (and reducing further the availability of jobs in agriculture), they did not take advantage of opportunities in commerce and industry at home, but invested instead in apartment buildings in New York or in condominiums in Florida. With the loss of land, the shrinkage of rural employment, and the decline in the quality of public services, the Costa Rican peasant faces a gloomy future, indeed. One-quarter of the Costa Rican population is poor, but 75 percent of the poor are in rural areas.

The Costa Rican peasant is accustomed to poverty; perhaps that is why he has endured this long, but there may be a breaking point. Mitchell Seligson (1980) suggests that the lack of unrest may be attributed to the fact that the changes have been gradual. He warns that an accumulation of factors may be catching up with Costa Rica. In the past, the growth of agrarian capitalism, as Seligson calls it, provided a number of "escape valves." Even when the peasant lost his land, he might find employment (and perhaps an improved standard of living) on the coffee *fincas* or banana plantations. There was also the possibility of migration, but this option existed only as long as there was a frontier. Today, with the proliferation of cattle spreads and *milpas*, the frontier has disappeared. Wasteful farming has caused deforestation and consequent soil erosion, compounding the peasant's plight. In 1950, 72 percent of Costa Rica was forest, but this cover has indeed dwindled to 34 percent in 1977, raising the specter of ecological disaster in Costa Rica. Seligson adds that another factor militating against peasant revolt is the homogeneity of the population. Unlike Mexico and Guatemala, where the peasants are also members of a conquered race, Costa Rica does not have a racial context to its peasant problem; this, he believes, accounts for the lack of repression and of the disposition to avoid force. The peasants are still free individuals, and the egalitarian spirit tempers the resort to violence on all sides.

The central government has not been oblivious to the problems of the rural sector and has tried to assist the municipalities by providing schools, health and sanitation facilities, roads, and electrification, but a national government, particularly one lacking in overall planning and resources, cannot be everywhere at once, and remoteness tends to obscure needs. In 1949, the central government attempted to promote agriculture through the creation of the National Council of Production (CNP). The purpose of the CNP, as described earlier, was to establish price stability for farm products by means of rational marketing. The CNP built silos for the storage of the grains and beans that it purchased at a fixed price or held under a system of credits, in order to overcome the fluctuation of prices caused either by a scarcity or surplus. It also established powdered-milk plants and cold-storage lockers for the same purpose. This effort aided agriculture, but benefited the large producers more than the peasants. Eventually, the CNP became an agribusiness in its own right, much to the dismay of the private sector.

The Institute of Lands and Colonization (ITCO), created in 1961, provided more direct aid to the peasant. However, the reluctance of *tico* leaders to acknowledge that they had a land-distribution problem undermined ITCO's effectiveness. Initially, it adopted a policy of colonizing new lands, which it later abandoned when it concluded that the investment in resources greatly exceeded the returns. Next, it tried a program of helping peasants to acquire title to their land, both those who had been on the land for generations and recent squatters. This program was only a piecemeal one at best and, in a number of cases, was counter-productive, as unscrupulous land agents in San José exploited the law to their advantage in the courts. In recent times, peasants, showing a restiveness, have organized land invasions, occasionally with the support of ITCO, and have acquired title to the land. ITCO, slowly becoming more aggressive, has placed a cap on the size of landholdings, which has forced some land redistribution. None of these measures has significantly improved the status of the Costa Rican peasant so far. When other escape valves seemed to fail, the peasant could move to the city, but this option is quickly disappearing.

The flight of the peasants to the urban centers of the Meseta Central has stimulated an urbanization process that is placing severe strains upon the *tico* economy. Approximately one-fourth of the Costa Rican population lives in the metropolitan area of San José, and the figure soars to 61 percent of the population when one includes the entire Meseta Central. If the trend in rural-to-urban migration continues, OFIPLAN predicts that 86 percent of the Costa Rican population will be urban by the year 2000 and that 91 percent of this concentration will be in the Meseta Central. The rapid growth of the public sector, industrialization, and the heavy allocation of resources to the San José area have brought the peasants flocking to the city. Even now, as the bonanza days are disappearing, the attractions that the city holds for the peasant and other migrants are still strong. Jobs may be scarce and housing inadequate, but there are better schools, health-care facilities, utilities, and public assistance agencies than the peasant ever knew in the villages. The contrast between the public services available in the urbanized Meseta and what exists in the rural regions is startling. For example, the Costa Rican Institute of Aqueducts and Sewers (ICAA) estimated that in 1978, 93 percent of the population of the metropolitan area of San José received good-quality drinking water, whereas in areas of concentrated rural population (towns of 200 to 2,000 inhabitants), comprising one-half of the rural population, 89 percent received service, but the quantity and quality of water was judged "inadequate, in general" (OFIPLAN, 1980). Of the other half of the rural population, designated as dispersed, 60 percent received no drinking water from the ICAA or any other governmental agency.

For 30 years, the major investment in the welfare state has been in the Meseta. Metropolitan San José has indeed outstripped the rest of the nation, not merely out of selfishness, but as a practical matter. The bureaucratic bourgeoisie demanded and received roads, transportation, and utilities; as a compact area, the Meseta developed infrastructure with relative ease. It was more costly to extend the power lines, sewers, aqueducts, and telephones outside the economic boundary of the capital city. As the slums of San José grew, the city dwellers knew they had a problem, and the National Institute of Housing and Urban Development (INVU) was created in 1954 to solve it. In 1975, a study by Rodrigo Carreras and Charles Denton, among others (OFIPLAN, 1980), determined that there were 76,939 substandard housing units in Costa Rica, which it described as either poor (lacking commodes, water, and electricity) or overcrowded. Of these, 42,789 were located in the Meseta Central; but all 76 construction firms in Costa Rica were also located in the metropolitan area, indicating where the work was being done. President Figueres established the Combined Institute of Social Assistance (IMAS) in 1971, which dealt with extreme poverty, providing uniforms and meals for school children and payments for families, to keep children in school. IMAS also engaged in slum clearance, because INVU was not set up to take care of the extremely poor. These were national programs instituted by the central government, but, in much the same manner as the hospitals and clinics of the social security system, an unequal share of the services has been performed in the metropolitan area. In many respects, at least until very recently, the urban poor have lived better than the poor of the rural areas. At the same time, the social problems that accompany urban poverty are relatively new to Costa Rica.

Aside from the fact that the urbanized Meseta Central is absorbing most of the public expenditures in services and welfare, urbanization is creating other economic and social problems. The concentration of population there results in heavy use of roads, public transportation, and utilities, so mere maintenance costs, much less new services, take a large bite out of the national budget. This situation exists primarily because municipal government, even in the cantons of San José, is weak, and local revenues are virtually nonexistent. National agencies provide the services, and national revenues, principally from import duties and export taxes, pay for them. Costa Rica has an income tax, but evasion is the rule rather than the exception. The better-paid workers of the Meseta, who use most of the services, avoid paying for them, except where there is direct billing, as in the case of electricity.

Crowded housing and traffic congestion are taking their toll on the once easygoing manner of the *ticos*. Crime, prostitution, drug addiction, and alcoholism are increasing at alarming rates, and *tico* society has been slow to develop the institutions to deal with them. In the past, crime was such an aberration that criminals were locked away in primitive prisons and virtually forgotten. Today, *ticos* are becoming aware of the more complex factors that may contribute to criminal activity and are proposing the construction of new correctional facilities, with an emphasis upon rehabilitation. However, police training and attitudes are backward, and courts are disposed more toward punishment than justice. The Rio Torres and Rio Aguilar, which wind through San José, are open sewers, and squatter shacks line the debris-ridden banks. Industrial wastes and toxic chemicals are new elements of the Meseta's air and water pollution, which go unchecked without adequate ordinances, zoning, and policing. Metropolitan San José has the same problems as many of the rapidly expanding cities of the developing world, but *ticos* have been slow to realize that it might be better to develop programs to enable peasants to remain on the land, rather than pouring resources into the city and making it the only place to be. Part of the cause of this problem is the Costa Rican political system, which seems unable to take corrective measures.

Political power in Costa Rica is widely dispersed, so instead of simply being a system of checks and balances, the process is one of deadlock. In their desire to curb presidential power, the *ticos* have tethered the president. Despite the constitutional restrictions, there are many ways in which a strong-willed president can exercise influence — through personal persuasion and informal contacts, party control, and the authority to issue decrees — but even the most forceful is limited by the lack of budgetary discretion and by the restriction to a single term. The single term may rule out the *caudillo*, but the degree of corruption in the last three administrations indicates that it may be creating a problem just as serious. Clearly, the single term runs the risk of exhausting the pool of talented leaders. Although many *ticos* remain committed to the principle of no reelection, sentiment is growing for reverting to the former practice of permitting a president to run again after a hiatus of eight years, or for extending the presidential term from four to six years. Whatever formula is adopted, the main problem of the presidency is its lack of control or authority over the bureaucracy.

The autonomous institutions are too autonomous. They grew up over a period of time so as to meet specific needs, without central planning or coordination, but, once created, became self-perpetuating. A number continued after the need was gone, or assumed new functions not originally intended for them. Some institutions, such as the Central Bank and the Costa Rican Institute of Electricity (ICE), perform effectively and usefully, while others are a waste and duplication, but both kinds have successfully resisted pressures by the executive and legislative branches. Presidents have tried to establish a new level of institutions that can serve as umbrellas or coordinating agencies (e.g., OFIPLAN, DINADECO, and the Institute for Municipal Development and Consultation [IFAM]), but with limited success. In fact, some agencies continue to exist even when a new president creates another coordinating agency of his own. For example, Carazo expanded the presidential staff, particularly the Office of Information of the Presidential House, and charged it with the preparation of planning documents. But OFIPLAN, inaugurated by Oduber, remains active, so Carazo appears to have duplicated the planning function. Nonetheless, these agencies are confined largely to making recommendations, so projects that are dependent upon the cooperation of the myriad of central-government ministries and autonomous institutions must rely principally upon persuasion, while the ICE or ICAA, for example, may have already established projects and priorities of their own. The budgetary power, the one strong element of persuasion, resides in the Legislative Assembly, but it is unable to exercise it effectively, because the National Bureau of the Budget is itself an autonomous agency.

While the Legislative Assembly is the strongest branch of government, weaknesses inherent in its structure have rendered it sterile. The most serious deficiency is the prohibition of reelection. As Alberto Cañas (1978) says, "we punish experience." While the system may root out deadwood and prevent the development of entrenched interests, it does not permit legislators to develop the experience and expertise to deal with the increasingly complex and technical problems of modern society. Instead of being representative and powerful, as the constitution intended, the deputies, who do not have to worry about facing their constituents again, place greater emphasis upon self-enrichment than upon public service. They are susceptible to influence by political parties, as they hope for future employment in the ministries or agencies of the government, or are vulnerable to private or vested interests, which are also potential employers. National interests take precedence over local needs, accelerating the urban-rural disparity; and the young lawyer from Puntarenas, who uses his term in office to make contacts, normally sets up his practice in San José after his term is over, and never returns to Puntarenas. The system gives inordinate political power to organized interests and pressure groups, causing a further decline in the influence of the popular sectors. The autonomous agencies, as a pressure group, influence legislation favorable to their interests, and, once this is accomplished, the bureaucrats, organized in a union, walk off with the lion's share of the benefits, by threatening to strike unless they receive better wages. The low-income or poor families (those earning less than ₡1,500, or $176, a month in 1979), who constitute 40 percent of the population, are underrepresented and are increasingly being pushed to the margins of political power.

The PLN, primarily, has modernized Costa Rican society and promoted the rise of a middle class, but Francisco Morales, the minister of labor under Figueres, feels that the middle-class model of development has reached "the end of the line" (Morales, 1978). He argues that the mixed-economy/welfare-state strategy has exhausted its solutions and that it is now generating a new concentration of wealth. In his opinion, the challenge to Costa Rica in the 1980s is to incorporate the popular classes in political affairs and development. OFIPLAN agrees with this analysis, claiming that the decision-making process is concentrated in the hands of the traditional, paternalistic sectors, which represent essentially the urban areas. OFIPLAN insists that Costa Rica must provide meaningful political participation for a larger number of *ticos*, calling for grass-roots development and the exercise of power at the community level. Morales believes that political parties must be strengthened as a way to combat pressure groups and vested interests and to preserve democracy, but many observers charge that the PLN has become a middle-class party and has abandoned its original purposes. Put another way, the PLN appears satisfied with what it has achieved and is ignoring the needs of those still left out, which does not augur well for it or for Costa Rica. The most severe critics declare that the "reformist state" can no longer conceal the defects of capitalism, and speak darkly of the need for "genuine revolution."

Tico democracy has many problems, including its serious balance-of-payments deficit, a weakened economy supporting a broad public sector, a self-seeking bureaucracy, an alarming level of poverty, a disparity in the allocation of resources between urban and rural sectors, and an immobilized political system. On the latter point, Guido Fernández, the former editor of *La Nación*, notes that Costa Rica has built a state mechanism to provide extensive economic and social services, but has decentralized it politically in order to protect individual freedom. "We have the worst of two systems," he affirms (Fernández, 1978). The *ticos* need to devise the means by which they can transform their cherished freedoms into effective political action. They fear that what happened to Uruguay could happen to them. Time is running out for Costa Rica. Many of its problems are caused by external economic factors beyond its control, but, given its limited resources, one part of the population cannot continue to ride the back of the other part, without making sacrifices of its own. If the existing political system cannot do this, it needs to be reformed, or else the crisis will worsen, and the opportunity for change *a la tica* will be diminished.

7

CONCLUSION: TODAY AND TOMORROW

Costa Rica has a reputation as a model democracy, and one runs the risk, in enumerating its problems, of being accused of trying to create interest through sensationalism. Let it be understood that Costa Rica's problems are serious, and the crisis is real, but the discussion of them springs more from hope than desperation. The hope arises from Costa Rica's history, the character of its people, and the legitimacy of its institutions. Moreover, one learns about Costa Rica's problems principally from Costa Rican sources. *Ticos* are aware of the troubles in their society, because a free press writes about them, and its political leaders agonize about them in public forums. *Ticos* cherish their freedom, above all else. In late 1980, former President Figueres suggested suspending the constitution and creating an emergency government – composed of President Carazo, the four living ex-presidents, and the five leading candidates for the presidency in 1982 – with full executive and legislative power to do what was necessary until the crisis passed. He received no support for his proposal. As long as *ticos* know what is wrong, and there is no repressive apparatus in place to maintain the status quo, they are not going to panic and lose what they have.

Charles Denton (1971) wonders if the *ticos* can afford such tranquillity, given the magnitude of their problems. *Ticos* have resorted to violence in the past, when they had a tyrant to blame and overthrow. Now, they face a situation that they themselves have created over three decades, although it has been recently exacerbated by energy costs; and they believe that they can undo, within the same framework, what they have done. As Luis Alberto Monge said recently, "The ills of democracy can only be cured by democracy" (*New York Times*, Dec. 15, 1980). Admitting that they have made mistakes, *ticos* also believe that their democracy has achieved remarkable progress. Aware that a way must be found to give greater political participation to more people, most *ticos* are very proud of the extensive nature of the suffrage. Observers remark that the quality of life has declined and that the old ways are passing (which are really manifestations of urbanization and modernization), but *ticos* look at the statistics and note significant improvements, whether in literacy, infant survival, life expectancy, hospital beds, road construction, or telephones. Although Denton and others may express dismay over the tranquillity or apathy of the Costa Ricans, the *ticos* realize they have too much at stake to be seduced by supposedly quick-fix solutions.

Alberto Cañas (1978), a PLN founder, is concerned that the old traditions are disappearing and that youth is no longer motivated by former values. I have visited Costa Rica regularly since 1966 and would argue that Costa Rican culture seems more vital than ever. Fifteen years ago, there were no public exhibitions of paintings by Costa Ricans. Today, the works of Teodorico Quirós, Fausto Pacheco, and Francisco Amighetti, among others, may be viewed in the galleries of the National Insurance Institute (INS) and at the new Museum of Costa Rican Art, housed in the refurbished terminal building of the former La Sabana International Airport. Samuel Rovinski (1977) notes that when the Costa Rican government established a national publishing house (Editorial Costa Rica, [ECR]) in 1958, many persons regarded the support for a small group of "mediocre writers" as a waste of public funds. Today, ECR publishes 300 titles by Costa Rican writers annually, with 150,000 copies sold each year exclusively in Costa Rica. Although ECR receives public funds, its editorial board makes all publishing decisions, without interference by any governmental agency. One can readily attest to this by reviewing the large number of titles by authors representing every ideological position and critically analyzing all aspects of Costa Rican life in works of fiction and non-fiction. There is TV and the pop culture, but obviously *ticos* are reading, because, in addition to ECR, the three state universities maintain presses, and there are several private publishers as well. The advancement of Costa Rican culture and the attention to the problems of modern life received an additional boost with the creation of the Ministry of Culture, Youth, and Sports (MCJD) by President Figueres in 1972.

In his widely quoted comment, "Why tractors without violins?" (Ameringer, 1979), Figueres recognized the importance of cultural development alongside economic development. The MCJD has literally changed the Costa Rican landscape, through the development of the vast recreational and sports complex on the site of the old La Sabana Airport, and by using proceeds from newly established tree farms for the creation of the Young Peoples Orchestra and the revitalization of the National Symphonic Orchestra. A significant aspect of the MCJD's work is its emphasis upon serving the nation at large. Through its National Handicraft and Small Industry Program, it is preserving and stimulating popular arts, giving employment and new sources of income to rural artisans, and spurring cottage industries. Rovinski (1977) points out that the National Symphony now performs more frequently in the towns and villages of Costa Rica than in the National Theater in San José. In the same way, MCJD, with the support of DINADECO and IFAM, is promoting little theater groups in culturally deprived communities. Much of the credit for all this belongs to Cañas, who was the first minister of culture, youth, and sports. These actions alone are not going to stem the rural migration to the cities, but they are a beginning toward the improvement of rural life. This trend is also marked in OFIPLAN's *National Development Plan, 1979-82.*

OFIPLAN is troubled by the stagnation of agriculture, caused, it believes, by the heavy subsidization of the industrial sector. While it grapples with the problem of finding the appropriate mix of economic activity by the public and private sectors, it proposes to give local communities real power (political and economic) to solve their problems and end the so-called urban imperialism of San José. Seligson (1980) says that only a "determined effort" on the part of the state can "halt the demise of the peasant." There are indications that such an effort is intended for the 1980s. ICE is pushing rural electrification, and exciting plans are underway in the area of geothermal energy, utilizing the line of volcanos running from the Nicaraguan frontier in the northwest to the Meseta Central. The National Training Institute (INA) is endeavoring to teach peasants new skills required by mechanized agriculture and agri-business. The new highway extending from the Meseta to San Ramón (and soon to reach Puntarenas) is part of a plan to stimulate agricultural production in foodstuffs and other nontraditional products. There is no question that ITCO needs to be more aggressive and imaginative in the area of agrarian reform, but OFIPLAN is now committed to a program of land redistribution, and to a plan of economic expansion of agriculture that is projected to produce a rate of real growth at no less than 4 percent annually.

The stagnation of agriculture was not the only problem perceived by OFIPLAN in its *National Development Plan, 1979-1982.* In fact, it listed the following additional major problems confronting the nation:

- the chronic balance-of-payments problem;
- the growing foreign debt;
- the growing dependence on foreign nations – technological and cultural as well as financial;
- a foreign trade dependent upon the exportation of a limited number of products;
- uncertainty over the behavior of international markets, with reference to the products Costa Rica exports and those it imports;
- existence of a system of incentives and protectionism not adapted to actual needs;
- loss of the dynamism of the Central American Common Market;
- abuse in the exploitation of natural resources;
- concentration of economic, social, and political activities in the Meseta Central;
- a high proportion of the population living in a state of extreme poverty;
- entrenched state paternalism, which works against the strengthening of democracy;

• increase in alcoholism, prostitution, and the mistreatment and abandonment of children;

• an excessively large public sector, weighing too heavily upon the economy of the country;

• scarce participation by large sectors of the population in economic and political decisions.

Generally, the Carazo administration failed to attack effectively the problems it had identified, until it was too late. Specifically, it delayed any action until the decline in coffee prices and the increase in the cost of petroleum had made the chronic balance-of-payments problem an acute one. Underlying OFIPLAN's list of problems, which contains most issues touched upon in this study, was the reality that Costa Rica was spending more than it could afford. However, as long as the trade deficit remained reasonable, there was not sufficient political strength, or concern, to force a change in direction. From the manner in which OFIPLAN worded some of the problems — such as, "concentration of resources in the Meseta Central," "an entrenched state paternalism," and "an excessively large public sector" — it was clear that the Carazo administration was ideologically unsympathetic toward the welfare state. Yet, the administration was either unable or unwilling to advance beyond its rhetoric.

There are a number of possible explanations for this inertia. It has been suggested that the Costa Rican political system is immobilized: that the distinct branches of government are so evenly balanced as to produce a deadlock and to render it incapable of reforming itself. This argument, debatable in itself, seemed to acquire some force because Carazo's own political base was narrow and he had achieved election through a coalition of forces. It was difficult for him to fashion a coherent policy because of the competing groups within his own administration and the shifting voting blocs within the Legislative Assembly. Carazo himself proved to be a weak leader, lacking the vision to anticipate the growing economic problems and the courage to act upon his political convictions. The political system was immobilized because it was working reasonably well, and Carazo, despite evidence that changes were needed, was unwilling to disturb it. Carazo was not responsible for the decline in coffee prices, but he sensed that Costa Rican spending was creating a dangerous situation and he failed to act until events had overtaken him.

Toward the end of 1981, the Costa Rican economy was virtually bankrupt. As already noted, Costa Rica had a $670-million balance-of-payments deficit in 1980, which reflected a doubling in the price of oil the year before and a slump equally as large in the price of coffee. For a country dependent upon imported petroleum for as much as 50 percent of its energy needs and upon coffee for a similar proportion of its foreign earnings, such price changes were disastrous, whatever the political system. Equally as serious, the total external debt had risen to $2.6 billion, and in November 1981 Costa Rica was in danger of defaulting on the interest payments. This situation led to a 40-percent inflation rate, although by the end of 1981, most analysts claimed that the annual rate had reached 60 percent. Carazo devalued the *colón* by about one-half in 1980, but permitted it to float, so that its 1979 value of ₡8.60 to the dollar fell to about ₡40 to the dollar in early 1982. Carazo's sluggish action, in effect, left the *colón* overvalued too long, causing a run on Costa Rica's gold and dollar reserves and thereby compounding the monetary problem. Some experts predict that the *colón* will ultimately fall to 100 to 1, in terms of U.S. dollars. Costa Rica attempted to secure relief from its economic plight through the negotiation of a $330-million loan from the International Monetary Fund (IMF), extended over three years in equal amounts. The arrangement collapsed because Carazo would not undertake the austerity measures recommended by the IMF and imposed import restrictions that went against its advice.

Carazo refused to increase the cost to consumers for services and goods provided by state enterprises, such as electricity, water, and gasoline, thereby subsidizing, more than ever, a large portion of the economy. At the same time, he issued an emergency economic decree in November 1981 in which he threatened to prosecute individuals speculating in foreign exchange, established exchange controls, and restricted the importation of luxury items, including automobiles. He also entered into direct negotiations with Costa Rica's creditors, hoping, through a combination of moratoriums, new credits, and rescheduling of debt payments, to enable Costa Rica to make necessary reforms while maintaining solvency. The delay in completing these negotiations, plus Carazo's unwillingness to impose austerity measures, led to the suspicion that he was stalling until the 1982 elections and intended to leave the entire problem for the new administration to solve.

Despite the seriousness of Costa Rica's economic crisis, the nation's commitment to a democratic solution remained firm. Perhaps the fact that the crisis developed so close to the time for holding elections reinforced the willingness of *ticos* to go the electoral route. They perceived an imminent opportunity to make a change, particularly since they blamed their problems upon Carazo personally and were able to channel their discontent and frustrations into the activities of the campaign. To be sure, both of the principal candidates, Luis Alberto Monge Alvarez of the PLN, and Rafael Calderón Fournier of the Unity coalition, recognized the danger in raising the expectations of the Costa Rican people.

Monge (July 21, 1981) stressed that there was no "magic formula" for the solution of Costa Rica's problems. Moreover, as a committed social democrat and the author of legislation establishing the *aguinaldo*, he was in no position to attack the welfare state. Instead, he denounced the "mismanagement" of the economy by Carazo and emphasized the experience of the PLN in government and his own lengthy preparation for leadership. He had no intention of dismantling the public sector, but pledged to streamline it, to make it more efficient, to trim bureaucratic overhead, and to eliminate graft and corruption. He relied upon a general statement of principles (1981) entitled "Volvamos a la tierra" ("Let Us Return to the Land"), and prepared before the economic situation had worsened, in which he called for increased production, particularly in the agricultural sector. The main idea of returning to the land was not merely to stimulate agricultural production, but to recover "lost values" — a veiled attack upon state paternalism — while maintaining the state's role in providing basic services and in planning and development. Agriculture was seen as the area that could produce more food, earn more foreign capital, provide more jobs, develop new sources of energy (agroenergy), and achieve greater social justice and individual initiative through broader ownership of land (*Combate*, Feb. 1982). This was a long-range plan that did not confront the immediate problems, but as the campaign progressed, the outcome became so predictable that Monge and the PLN could afford to play it safe.

Principally, despite an early pledge to conduct a campaign of education and to address the issues, Monge and the PLN could not resist capitalizing upon the extreme unpopularity of Carazo. Under the circumstances, it was easier to talk about "a new dawn" than to risk losing votes by being too specific. Nor did Monge blame Costa Rica's economic problems on the international economic order, as Figueres had done consistently in the past, because that was also Carazo's argument. There was no wish to offend those whose assistance would probably be needed, especially when Carazo provided such a convenient target. Although certain Liberacionistas expressed disappointment with the United States for failing to aid Costa Rica, feeling that the Reagan administation was "punishing" it for its role in the overthrow of Somoza in Nicaragua, most believed it was highly unlikely, given the situation in Central America, that the United States would permit *tico* democracy to fail. Monge declared simply that he and his advisors would, in the 90 days between the election and his inauguration, devise an emergency plan of action, which would be put in place during his first 90 days in office. In the past, it had been Liberación against anti-Liberación. In the election of 1982, it was the PLN against Carazo, and there was little doubt as to who was going to win.

Rafael Calderón Fournier, Monge's principal opponent, faced overwhelming odds, compounded by the fact that he was in an ambiguous situation. He could not criticize the welfare state too vigorously because his father had been responsible for the bulk of the social reform in Costa Rica. He concentrated his attacks upon the economic programs of National Liberation, stressing the need to reduce the public sector and the degree of state intervention in the economy. The main thrust of his argument was the removal of the state from competition with the private sector, to encourage private investment, and to be compatible with the conservative aid programs being planned by the Reagan administration. Calderón's dilemma was that he was still the candidate of the Unity coalition and he could not divorce himself completely from Carazo and his unpopular government. At the same time, he was riding a dead horse because immediately after he received the nomination, the coalition began to fall apart. Only the deadline for printing the ballots finally forced Carazo's own Democratic Renovation Party to decide to remain in the coalition, whereas the Popular Union Party, representing the old oligarchy, actually withdrew during the week before the election. Calderón's principal hope was to maintain his credibility as a presidential candidate, because Unity itself was unlikely to survive the election, thereby postponing, for some time, Costa Rica's hope of evolving a two-party system.

Of the four other candidates in the presidential race, only two were significant, and none represented more than a protest vote. Former President Mario Echandi, the last of the ex-presidents eligible for reelection, entered the contest late as the standard bearer of what he called the National Movement Party. At 66, his appeal was largely a personalistic one and he ran on his reputation as a conservative, as an admirer of Ronald Reagan, and as a staunch anti-Communist. He sought to exploit the concern over terrorism and proclaimed simply, "Echandi or communism" (*The Tico Times* Jan. 29, 1982). Despite the fact that he was ineligible for advance public financing, he seemed to have sufficient financial backing (indicating where the coffee barons probably went) and attracted support from a mixed group of disgruntled politicians, including the erstwhile Liberacionista, Gonzalo Facio, who had abandoned plans for an independent candidacy. Although Echandi will remain active, his party will probably disappear. The other candidate of importance was Rodrigo Gutiérrez Sáenz, simply because he again represented United People, the coalition of Marxist parties. Gutiérrez conducted a spirited campaign, sensing an opportunity, owing to the current economic difficulties, to improve upon the 3-percent popular vote the coalition had obtained in 1978 and the three seats it had gained in the Assembly. United People appeared well financed and presented itself as the only real alternative to the old politics. It held an impressive rally in San José on February 4 (three days before the election), which attested as much to the strength of *tico* democracy as to the presence of communism in Costa Rica. Clearly, the Marxist parties remained united and were convinced that they had a future based on the belief that the economic situation would not improve. Gutiérrez took particular pains to disassociate himself from terrorist activity. The two remaining candidates, Edwin Chacón Madrigal of the Independent Party and Edwin Retana Chaves of the Democratic Party, did little more than keep these old party labels on the ballot. Not as colorful as the

1978 candidates of these parties, neither Chacón nor Retana aroused much interest or affected the outcome.

Observers remarked that the 1982 campaign was more quiet than any in recent times. Perhaps the economic crisis and the high cost of fuel restrained the *ticos'* enthusiasm. At least there were fewer autos racing down Avenida Central (the main thoroughfare of San José), honking horns and displaying party flags. Monge (1982) himself may have set the mood by declaring that the times dictated an "austere" campaign, although he affirmed that the economic difficulties would not "bend" the *ticos'* spirit. Interest may have flagged because the outcome was never in doubt, only the margin of victory. Some persons even suggested moving up the election day, in order to get it over with, but beneath the calm was a powerful sense of purpose. As Sunday, February 7, approached, the activity became more lively, and the autos, honking, and banners, indeed, appeared. On election day, a true carnival spirit prevailed, and the *ticos* warmed to their *fiesta cívica.* The polling places were surrounded by the youthful guides of the parties, who were dressed in party colors, leading cheers, and belying the existence of an economic crisis. The extreme good nature of the participants was admirable; there were no ugly episodes. Approximately 76 percent of the 1,261,127 registered voters exercised the franchise in a vigorous reaffirmation of their faith in democracy.

Much of the success of election day could be attributed to the performance of the Supreme Electoral Tribunal (TSE). It monitored the campaign and voting in a thoroughly professional manner. There was no question that Costa Rica had acquired the experience to conduct a free and fair election. Volunteer delegates from the TSE helped to oversee the polls, and its officials traveled from place to place to avoid any irregularities. By invitation, the Organization of American States sent observers, who also toured the polling places. The TSE had no need to censure the celebrants, because they were well behaved, but in case of need, it had the security forces in readiness under its complete jurisdiction. Moreover, the sale of alcoholic beverages was banned, not only on election day, but for 24 hours before and after. When the polls closed at 6 P.M., the judges of the TSE assembled to receive the reports electronically from the polling places. They had the most modern means of communication and computers at their disposal and began announcing the preliminary returns as they came in. Within a few hours, the sealed bags containing the actual ballots began arriving at the TSE headquarters for the subsequent official tally. As usual, Don Pepe Figueres had the last word. When casting his ballot, he proclaimed to reporters: "Costa Rica, be it poor or be it rich, will always be democratic" (*La Nación*, Feb. 8, 1982).

On February 7, 1982, Luis Alberto Monge Alvarez (LAMA, to his countrymen) and the PLN won a decisive victory. Monge secured 58.7 percent of the vote (564,422 votes), while Calderón got 33.6 percent, with the two extreme parties, Echandi on the right and Gutiérrez on the left, receiving 3.8 and 3.3 percent, respectively (see Figure 1). The returns for the other two were miniscule. It was the best showing of a winning presidential candidate since 1953, surpassing Figueres's 55 percent in 1970. Nonetheless, the vote for Calderón was greater than anticipated. His most ambitious pollsters had predicted 27 percent, with some projecting a share as low as 19 percent; so his political future may be bright. In the contest for the Legislative Assembly, the PLN won 33 seats, giving Monge an absolute majority (and only five short of a two-thirds majority). This majority will be extremely important in enabling him to develop a clear program and confront the serious issues facing Costa Rica. A factor in Carazo's difficulties was his lack of majority support in the Assembly. Even though United People gained a seat, its total of four will not be as important as the three it held previously, because they will no longer function as deciding or swing votes. Gutiérrez admitted as much, declaring that the coalition's deputies would not "play the numbers game," but would discharge an "educative" role, "denouncing and combating corruption" (*La Nación*, Feb. 8, 1982). Monge and the PLN cannot blame the political system if they fail to straighten out affairs, because the Costa Rican people, in effect, have unstuck the machinery.

A very important aspect of the 1982 election was the fact that the Costa Rican people were determined to demonstrate the vitality of their democratic process. In many respects, the form became the substance. Despite the 24-percent abstention rate (high for a Costa Rican election), the *ticos* had a sense of urgency about this election and a need to show to themselves and the world that it could be held normally and that this was the path they wished to follow in resolving their problems. The overwhelming victory of the PLN

Figure 1

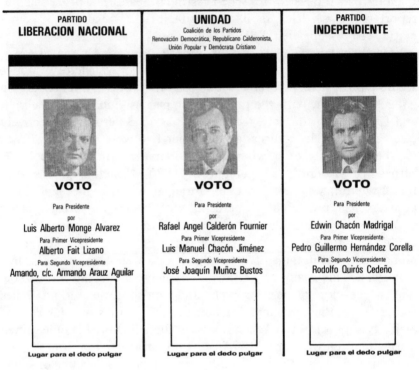

REPUBLICA DE COSTA RICA

ELECCIONES PARA PRESIDENTE Y

PARTIDO **LIBERACION NACIONAL**	**UNIDAD** Coalición de los Partidos Renovación Democrática, Republicano Calderonista, Unión Popular y Demócrata Cristiano	PARTIDO **INDEPENDIENTE**
VOTO	**VOTO**	**VOTO**
Para Presidente	Para Presidente	Para Presidente
por	por	por
Luis Alberto Monge Alvarez	Rafael Angel Calderón Fournier	Edwin Chacón Madrigal
Para Primer Vicepresidente	Para Primer Vicepresidente	Para Primer Vicepresidente
Alberto Fait Lizano	Luis Manuel Chacón Jiménez	Pedro Guillermo Hernández Corella
Para Segundo Vicepresidente	Para Segundo Vicepresidente	Para Segundo Vicepresidente
Amando, c/c. Armando Arauz Aguilar	José Joaquín Muñoz Bustos	Rodolfo Quirós Cedeño
Lugar para el dedo pulgar	Lugar para el dedo pulgar	Lugar para el dedo pulgar

Note: On the presidential ballot, the vote is recorded by means of a thumb-
In this way, even illiterate persons are able to vote in absolute secrecy.

Vote for president:*

Candidate	Total	Percentage
Monge	564,422	58.7
Calderón	323,105	33.6
Chacón	2,087	0.2
Echandi	36,635	3.8
Gutiérrez	31,772	3.3
Retana	1,922	0.2

VICEPRESIDENTES DE LA REPUBLICA 1982-1986

PARTIDO **MOVIMIENTO NACIONAL**	**PUEBLO UNIDO** Coalición de los Partidos Vanguardia Popular, Socialista Costarricense y de los Trabajadores	PARTIDO **DEMOCRATA**

VOTO

Para Presidente
por
Mario Echandi Jiménez
Para Primer Vicepresidente
Jaime Gutiérrez Góngora
Para Segundo Vicepresidente
José Joaquín Vargas Gené

Lugar para el dedo pulgar

VOTO

Para Presidente
por
Rodrigo Alberto Gutiérrez Sáenz
Para Primer Vicepresidente
José Joaquín Gutiérrez Mangel
Para Segundo Vicepresidente
Arnoldo Mora Rodríguez

Lugar para el dedo pulgar

VOTO

Para Presidente
por
Edwin Retana Chaves
Para Primer Vicepresidente
Jeannette Bolaños Paniagua
Para Segundo Vicepresidente
Alicia Soto Blanco

Lugar para el dedo pulgar

print in the box beneath the party banner and photograph of the candidate.

Seats won in the Legislative Assembly, by party:*

Party	Seats
National Liberation	33
Unity	18
United People	4
National Movement	1
Alajuelan Democratic Action	1

*Preliminary returns, with 99 percent of the vote counted.

was, in the same way, an expression of national unity. Monge and the PLN were being given the support necessary to confront Costa Rica's economic crisis, and it would be a mistake to interpret the results as the beginning of one-party rule. Monge, himself, proved gracious in victory and clearly understood its broader meaning. On the day after the election, in the traditional appearance of the president-elect on the steps of the Metropolitan Cathedral in the company of the archbishop, Monge asked the *ticos* to set aside their party banners and colors and to display now only the flag of Costa Rica. In this moment of good feeling, Monge received the additional good news that the price of coffee had increased 36 percent during the week before the election and that President Reagan planned to ask the U.S. Congress to approve $110 million in emergency aid for Costa Rica.

It is difficult to predict what kind of president Monge will be, because circumstances will probably not permit him to pursue the course he would prefer. He is more liberal and less disposed to follow U.S. initiatives than were recent Costa Rican presidents. Nonetheless, the economic crisis and the demands of creditors for austerity measures will restrict him in enlarging upon social programs. The prospect of relief from the United States will influence Monge to adapt Costa Rican foreign policy to the actions of the Reagan administration. These realities must be balanced against the record of Monge, who has been active in politics for 40 years.

Monge is more committed to social democracy than was any previous PLN president (Figueres, Orlich, or Oduber). He is not a landowner, as each of the others was, nor is he a man of means. His early experience was in the trade-union movement, in which he acknowledged a particular debt to the influence of Víctor Sanabria. He was Benjamín Núñez's lieutenant in the Rerum Novarum union of the 1940s and, when Núñez went into the hills to serve as Figueres's revolutionary chaplain in the 1948 civil war, Monge remained in San José to organize labor cadres into sabotage units for harassing the Calderonistas behind the lines. At age 23, he was a delegate to the Constituent Assembly and took part in the drafting of the constitution of 1949. (In the 1982 campaign, he reiterated his solemn commitment to the instrument he had helped to write.) During the formative period of the PLN and Figueres's first presidency (1953-58), Monge was involved in the Inter-American Regional

Organization of Labor (ORIT). ORIT was affiliated with the International Confederation of Free Trade Unions (ICFTU), based in Brussels, which, during the fifties, competed with the Communist-backed World Federation of Trade Unions (WFTU) for leadership of the international labor movement.

ORIT was concerned with the rights of free labor during a time when dictators dominated Latin America, particularly in the Caribbean. In this way, Monge became deeply involved in the anti-dictatorial struggle of the democratic left and collaborated with such figures as Serafino Romualdi of the American Federation of Labor and Norman Thomas of the Institute for International Labor Research (IILR). In 1956, Monge became secretary general of ORIT, with headquarters in Mexico City, where he aided numerous Caribbean exiles, including Castro and other Cubans involved in the overthrow of Batista. Through these activities and ORIT's connections with the ICFTU, Monge established contacts with social-democratic leaders of Latin America and Western Europe. Monge probably has more international experience than any previous Costa Rican president.

In 1959, when the PLN and other parties of the democratic left established the Inter-American Institute of Political Education (IIEP) in San José, Monge became the managing editor of its principal journal, *Combate*. He endeavored to make *Combate* a true medium of social-democratic thought in Latin America, soliciting articles from political leaders and intellectuals of Latin and North America and Western Europe. At this time, Monge was also a member of the board of directors of the IILR and he persuaded his fellow directors to provide financial assistance to the IIEP and *Combate*. Monge was unaware that the U.S. Central Intelligence Agency was using the IILR as a conduit for covert funding, but he soon perceived that the IILR, particularly its representative in San José, Sacha Volman, wanted to convert *Combate* into a propaganda instrument for attacking communism, rather than helping it develop into a sound intellectual organ of democratic expression and economic and social analysis, as conceived by Monge. The conflict between Monge and Volman led to the decision by the IILR to withdraw from Costa Rica and to create a new Center for Democratic Education in Mexico City, directly under the control of Volman, and to begin publication of another journal, *Panoramas*, under the editorship of Víctor Alba. Monge's own anticommunism was firm, but he complained bitterly to Figueres that the North Americans only wanted to use the Latins for a "McCarthy-style" fight against communism and that they had the preconceived notion that all Latins were "shameless and bums" (Ameringer, 1979). Eventually, Monge was able to reorganize the IIEP as the Inter-American School of Democratic Education, with funding from the Frederich Ebert Foundation of the Social Democratic Party of West Germany. This arrangement further demonstrated Monge's contacts with European social-democratic circles, which also included a closer relationship during the sixties with Albert Carthy of the Socialist International.

Nonetheless, the collapse of *Combate* depressed Monge greatly. Despite the fact that the Orlich administration appointed him ambassador to Israel in 1963 (Monge was much impressed with the similarities between Costa Rica and Israel and looked upon Israel as a model for development), Monge became disillusioned with Orlich and felt that he had abandoned the goals of the PLN. In August 1963, he accused Orlich of engaging in a campaign of "McCarthyism" (a favorite term of Monge's) against the liberal wing of National Liberation, and he told Figueres that he would resign from the party unless Figueres made a statement on radio and television denouncing these tactics (Ameringer, 1979). Figueres managed to calm Monge, expressing concern over his state of mind, and persuaded him to take a furlough from active politics. In addition to his political disappointments, Monge was experiencing a number of personal problems at the time and he went to Mexico for about a year, where his son underwent a surgical operation, financed by Figueres.

When Monge returned to Costa Rica in the mid-sixties, he became the secretary general of the PLN and undertook the reorganization of the party. The defeat of Oduber in 1966 placed strains upon the party, which Monge attributed to its domination by the three principal leaders − or "troika" − Figueres, Orlich, and Oduber. He sought to overcome personalism in the PLN and to reestablish it as a permanent ideological party. In 1970, he functioned as a mediator between Oduber and Figueres. Oduber felt he should have a second chance, as Orlich had gotten after his defeat in 1958, but Figueres was convinced that only he himself could revive the party's fortunes. Monge fashioned an agreement whereby

Figueres got the nomination in 1970, with the understanding that Oduber would receive it in 1974. These years as party secretary matured Monge, bestowing upon him the skills of a practical politician and an appreciation of the need to develop the PLN institutionally.

Monge's presidency will probably be greatly influenced by the experience he gained in running the daily affairs of the PLN for almost 15 years. Although he does not have the charisma of a Figueres and prefers a three-piece suit to shirt-sleeves, he knows the party and its people intimately. Unlike recent presidents, he may be able to secure the cooperation of the Legislative Assembly, because he has worked with most of the PLN deputies and he knows their constituencies. He is not an "Avenida Central" politician (San José oriented), but has traveled throughout Costa Rica, striving to promote local organization. Moreover, Monge has had two terms as a deputy in the Legislative Assembly (1958-62 and 1970-74), serving as its president during the second period. As noted, the current economic problems will probably check his ideological proclivities, particularly since U.S. policy will be a consideration in any recovery program, and since the Reagan administration is lukewarm toward the social-democratic course. Monge has a record of opposing communism in Latin America, but, as he stated many times, it was not a negative approach, but, rather, a belief in the need for democracy to promote economic and social change in order to eradicate the conditions the Communists might exploit.

In this regard, he is likely to continue the close ties he has developed with Social- and Christian-Democratic parties in Latin America and Europe. (Interestingly, only two days after his election, Monge received a delegation of Democratic Action [AD] leaders from Venezuela, including Jaime Lusinchi, AD's presidential nominee for the 1983 elections.) Monge's experience with North Americans, even liberals, during the sixties was not pleasant. He sought to improve relations with the social-democratic movements of Western European and even with the Socialist International. The international policy of the PLN and Costa Rican foreign policy itself will be more attuned to Latin American and European initiatives than to those of the United States, although, as noted, U.S. aid will be a modifying factor. Moreover, events in Nicaragua and the rest of Central America will be of concern to Monge and the *ticos*. The public revulsion against acts of terrorism in 1981, and evidence that the Cubans used their consulate in San José for gunrunning activities during the Nicaraguan fighting (leading to a suspension of Costa Rican-Cuban consular relations in May 1981), will have a strong influence on foreign policy. Monge does not want the Sandinistas to take over Nicaragua any more than the United States does, but he can be expected to argue that the best means of preventing that from happening is by supporting the democratic elements in Nicaragua, rather than by cutting off all aid to Nicaragua and assuming a threatening attitude toward the Sandinistas. During the late stages of the campaign, however, the PLN assumed a noticeably strident anti-Communist stance. Only time will tell whether or not this was campaign rhetoric, but one senses that the position has, indeed, hardened. The unstable conditions in Central America, along with the domestic economic malaise, pose serious threats to Costa Rican democracy.

The challenges facing Monge's administration will be among the most serious in Costa Rican history. Many *ticos* have already expressed a fear about the "Uruguayan nightmare." Two months before the election, the *New York Times* (Dec. 11, 1981) quoted a "liberal politician" as saying, "If we had an army, we'd have had a coup d'etat by now." The fact that Costa Rica does not have an army may be one reason why there will be no repetition of the Uruguayan experience. Although *ticos* see an analogy between Costa Rica and Uruguay, noting that Uruguay was once a model democracy with advanced social and economic programs, Uruguay has a strong military tradition, which Costa Rica never had. In the late nineteenth century, during the so-called era of professional soldiers, the Uruguayan military brought an end to the violence raging in that country and established the foundation for the democratic state and the social and economic reforms that were to follow. Moreover, Uruguay has always been concerned about its security, owing to the aggressive designs of its two large neighbors, Argentina and Brazil. In fact, Brazil's objection to radical movements in Uruguay during the sixties probably had a hand in the fall of Uruguayan democracy.

Costa Rica's neighbors are not as intimidating, nor has Costa Rica experienced the intense urban guerrilla activity and terrorism that preceded the collapse of Uruguayan democracy. The actions of the Tupamaros in Uruguay undermined the civilian government and provided the opportunity for the military takeover. Serious terrorist groups have yet to appear in Costa Rica, and the general aversion of *ticos* toward violence makes it unlikely that they would be tolerated, much less win acceptance. Despite its vulnerability to violent action and the presence of militant exile groups, Costa Rica is not fertile ground for those who would resort to arms. The extremists at both ends of the political spectrum may cause a commotion, but *ticos* have traditionally shunned extremes. Aware that the danger from the right may be as great as that from the left, *ticos* have rebuffed recent U.S. suggestions that they strengthen their security forces. The real test lies in the ability of the system to reform itself.

Monge and the PLN are aware that the greatest similarity between their situation and that of Uruguay before the fall is the existence of the welfare state, with its heavy dependence upon a few agricultural products. Costa Rica, like Uruguay formerly, suffers from low productivity and a large bureaucracy and state mechanism. Monge and the PLN recognize that the welfare state is running a huge deficit and they resent the abuses of the bureaucratic bourgeoisie. Their dilemma is how to make reforms without abandoning their fundamental beliefs. Social democracy is on trial and the problem does become one of ideology. Can Monge and the PLN change their course, if necessary, after having been committed to it for over 30 years? Uruguay apparently could not, but perhaps the lesson of its failure to do so might be another reason why Costa Rica will avoid a similar fate.

If Costa Rica's economic situation continues to deteriorate, it is likely that various groups, such as labor unions and peasant leagues, will begin to organize more seriously in defense of their interests, challenging the existing political-party structure. For the time being, Monge and the PLN are enjoying the unity produced by the 1982 election, but popularity erodes quickly, and hard times will cause defections. These defections may alter the style of political activity, but the situation will have to get a great deal worse before *ticos* abandon the electoral route. The majority of *ticos* will give LAMA a chance, at least for six months, before they begin thinking about elections again and start preparing for 1986. That is the *tico* way.

BIBLIOGRAPHY

Aguilar Bulgarelli, Oscar. *Costa Rica y sus hechos políticos de 1948. Problemático de una década.* San José: Editorial Costa Rica, 1969.

____. *La Constitución de 1949. Antecedentes y proyecciones.* 2d ed. San José: Editorial Costa Rica, 1974.

American University. *Area Handbook for Costa Rica.* Washington, D.C.: Foreign Area Studies, 1970.

Ameringer, Charles D. *The Democratic Left in Exile: The Antidictatorial Struggle in the Caribbean, 1945-1959.* Coral Gables: University of Miami Press, 1974.

____. *Don Pepe: A Political Biography of José Figueres of Costa Rica.* Albuquerque: University of New Mexico Press, 1979.

Araya Pochet, Carlos. *Historia de los partidos políticos: Liberación Nacional.* San José: Editorial Costa Rica, 1968.

Arias Sánchez, Oscar. *Grupos de presión en Costa Rica.* San José: Editorial Costa Rica, 1971.

____. *Nuevos rumbos para el desarrollo Costarricense.* San José: Editorial Universitaria Centroamericana, 1979.

____. *Quién gobierna en Costa Rica?.* 2d ed. San José: Editorial Universitaria Centroamericana, 1978.

Baker, Christopher E.; Fernández Pinto, Ronald; and Stone, Samuel Z. *Municipal Government in Costa Rica: Its Characteristics and Functions.* San José: Associated Colleges of the Midwest Central American Field Program and School of Political Science of the University of Costa Rica, 1972.

129

Barahona Jiménez, Luis. *El pensamiento político en Costa Rica*. San José: Editorial Fernández-Arce, 1971.

Bell, John Patrick. *Crisis in Costa Rica. The 1948 Revolution*. Austin: University of Texas Press, 1971.

Biesanz, Mavis Hiltunen; Biesanz, Richard; and Biesanz, Karen Zubris. *Los Costarricenses*. San José: Editorial Universidad Estatal a Distancia, 1979.

Blanco Segura, Ricardo. *Monseñor Sanabria*. San José: Editorial Costa Rica, 1971.

Busey, James L. *Notes on Costa Rican Democracy*. Boulder: University of Colorado Press, 1962.

Cañas, Alberto F. *Los 8 Años*. San José: Editorial Liberación Nacional, 1955.

_____ . "Alberto F. Cañas," *Ideario Costarricense/1977*, no. 7, "Régimen Político-Electoral." San José: Casa Presidencial, Oficina de Información, 1978.

Cerdas Cruz, Rodolfo. *La crisis de la democracia liberal en Costa Rica. Interpretación y perspectiva*. 2d ed. San José: Editorial Universitaria Centroamericana, 1975.

Combate. Organo oficial del partido Liberación Nacional.

Costa Rica. Casa Presidencial, Oficina de Información. *Ideario Costarricense/ 1977*, no. 5, "Burocracia Estatal." San José, 1977.

_____ . *Ideario Costarricense/1977*, no. 7, "Régimen Político-Electoral," San José, 1978.

Denton, Charles F. *Patterns of Costa Rican Politics*. Boston: Allyn and Bacon, 1971.

Díaz, Hugo. *El Mundo de Hugo Díaz*. San José: Editorial Costa Rica, 1978.

English, Bert H. *Liberación Nacional in Costa Rica: The Development of a Political Party in a Transitional Society*. Gainesville: University of Florida Press, 1971.

Fernández, Guido. "Guido Fernández," *Ideario Costarricense/1977*, no. 7. "Régimen Político-Electoral." San José: Casa Presidencial, Oficina de Información, 1978.

Figueres, José. *La pobreza de las naciones*. San José: Imprenta Nacional, 1974.

Gamboa, Francisco. *Costa Rica: ensayo histórico*. San José: Ediciones Revolución, 1971.

Goldrich, Daniel. *Sons of the Establishment: Elite Youth in Panama and Costa Rica*. Chicago: Rand McNally, 1966.

Institute for the Comparative Study of Political Systems. *Costa Rica: Election Factbook, February 6, 1966*. Washington, D.C.: Operations and Policy Research, Inc., 1966.

Kantor, Harry. *Patterns of Politics and Political Systems in Latin America*. Chicago: Rand McNally, 1969.

Monge, Luis Alberto. *Liberación Nacional está prepardo para afrontar la crisis nacional*. (Campaign address, July 21, 1981). San José: PLN, 1981.

_____ . *La Política de la Verdad*. (Campaign leaflet). San José: PLN, 1982.

Monge Alfaro, Carlos. *Historia de Costa Rica*. 14th ed. San José: Imprenta Trejos, 1976.

Morales, Francisco. "Francisco Morales," *Ideario Costarricense/1977*, no 7, "Régimen Político-Electoral," San José: Casa Presidencial, Oficina de Información, 1978.

OFIPLAN (Oficina de Planificación Nacional y Política Económica). *Plan Nacional de Desarrollo, 1979-1982*. San José, 1980.

Rodríguez Vega, Eugenio. *Los días de Don Ricardo*. San José: Editorial Costa Rica, 1971.

Rovinski, Samuel. *Cultural Policy in Costa Rica*. Paris: UNESCO, 1977.

Seligson, Mitchell A. *Peasants of Costa Rica and the Development of Agrarian Capitalism*. Madison: University of Wisconsin Press, 1980.

Stone, Samuel. *La dinastía de los conquistadores. La crisis del poder en la Costa Rica contemporánea.* San José: Editorial Universitaria Centroamericana, 1975.

Suñol, Julio. *Robert Vesco compra una república.* San José: Imprenta Trejos, 1974.

Zelaya, Chester (ed.). *Democracia en Costa Rica? Cinco opiniones polémicas.* 2nd ed. San José: Editorial Universidad Estatal a Distancia, 1979.

INDEX

ABOUT THE AUTHOR

Charles D. Ameringer is professor of Latin American History at the Pennsylvania State University. He is the author of *The Democratic Left in Exile: The Antidictatorial Struggle in the Caribbean, 1945-1959* (Miami, 1974) and *Don Pepe: A Political Biography of José Figueres of Costa Rica* (New Mexico, 1979), along with numerous articles in leading scholarly journals, including *The American Historical Review, The Hispanic American Historical Review,* and the *Journal of Inter-American Studies and World Affairs.* He completed his baccalaureate studies at the University of Wisconsin in 1949 and earned the Ph.D. degree at the Fletcher School of Law and Diplomacy in 1958.